ALL FOR JESUS

— A DEVOTIONAL —

FRANKLIN GRAHAM

WITH ROSS RHOADS

NELSON BOOKS
A Division of Thomas Nelson Publishers
Since 1798

www.thomasnelson.com

Published in Nashville, Tennessee, by Thomas Nelson, Inc.

Nelson Books titles may be purchased in bulk for educational, business, fundraising, or sales promotional use. For information, please email SpecialMarkets@ThomasNelson.com.

Library of Congress Cataloging-in-Publication Data

Graham, Franklin, 1952–
    All for Jesus : a devotional / Franklin Graham with Ross Rhoads.
      p. cm.
    Includes bibliographical references.
    ISBN 0-7852-6482-5 (hardcover)
    ISBN 0-7852-7394-8 (softcover)
    1. Jesus Christ—Prayer-books and devotions—English.
I. Rhoads, Ross, 1932– II. Title.
BT306.53.G73 2004
242—dc22   2003020049

Printed in the United States of America
05 06 07 08 09 RRD 5 4 3 2 1

To the Billy Graham Evangelistic Association
Crusade Staff and Team Members

CONTENTS

PART III

DISCIPLESHIP: BEYOND THE BASICS

PART IV

ASSURANCE: THE CERTAINTIES OF OUR FAITH

PART I

SERVICE:

GOD CAN USE

ANYONE

I AM YOUR GOD

Now Moses was tending the flock of Jethro his father-in-law, the priest of Midian, and he led the flock to the far side of the desert and came to Horeb, the mountain of God. There the angel of the LORD appeared to him in flames of fire from within a bush. Moses saw that though the bush was on fire it did not burn up. So Moses thought, "I will go over and see this strange sight—why the bush does not burn up."

When the LORD saw that he had gone over to look, God called to him from within the bush, "Moses, Moses!"

And Moses said, "Here I am."

"Do not come any closer," God said. "Take off your

sandals, for the place where you are standing is holy ground."
Then he said, "I am the God of your father, the God of
Abraham, the God of Isaac and the God of Jacob." At this,
Moses hid his face, because he was afraid to look at God.
(Exodus 3:1–6)

After forty years in the wilderness, Moses must have found the contrast of his new surroundings shocking. Wind blew sand, like a whirling tornado, stinging his face. The heat from the sun-baked earth radiated through his sandals. The relentless glare of the sun burned his face.

Try to imagine what Moses was thinking as he stood in the desert. He must have reminisced for years about how rich the soil was in Egypt compared to the arid flatlands of the desert. And how varied were the many delicacies of the royal menu and the fine oils that daily soothed his skin.

Now he is standing in a dry sea of sand with cracked lips, a bronzed face, and memories. At eighty years old, did he think, *This is the way I'm going to die?* And he certainly reflected on the events that brought him to that place.

Sometimes, when life mellows us, the things that are the saddest surface in our minds. We all think about the might-have-beens or the should-have-dones. We think about the personal scars that are less visible. As the desert sand scratched his face, perhaps Moses thought about how he had clawed in the sand, digging the hole to bury the Egyptian he had murdered.

Try to sense what Moses must have been feeling. It was just a regular day as he was standing in the desert, shielding his eyes from the sun—when suddenly, a nearby shrub began to burn. Turning to look, he noticed that it didn't burn up. It probably wasn't a large bush, being in the desert, so, by the time he came closer, the flame should have died out, but it didn't.

The angel of the Lord appeared in that flame, and as Moses stared at the bush, God called his name. We might wonder if Moses said to himself, *Who knows my name? My father-in-law doesn't care about my name. I married his daughter and I'm a good son-in-law and I'm working for him, but other than that, who really is thinking about me? Even God has forgotten me.*

Do you ever feel that way?

"Moses, Moses!" Moses went further to get a better look, but God said, "Stop right there! Don't come any closer. Not another step. Take off your sandals because the place where you're standing is holy ground."

Moses wanted to see how the bush was not consumed and understand what seemed impossible. We too want to understand the how's and why's of God's work though they are often kept from us as a mystery. The value and purpose of following God's ways are not in seeing but in believing what God wants to say to us. "Blessed are those," Jesus said to Thomas, "who have not seen and yet have believed" (John 20:29). Don't rely on your senses alone to interpret what is happening in your life. There is always a deeper meaning.

We should pause in order to note that Moses was in isolation when he met God at the bush. It's good to be isolated at times—our Lord was. Scripture tells us that Jesus went out alone a great while before daylight to pray. Far too many of us don't have enough alone time. We often become mentally and spiritually barren because we're so busy. Moses was certainly experiencing more alone than he had learned in the activity of the palace, and his solitude provided the perfect setting for God to speak.

In that inexplicable moment, God made a powerful statement to Moses. "I am the God of your father." What? After Moses was just a couple of years old, he never saw his father again. Without his parents, he grew up and was educated in a foreign culture. Moses had no family identity now; he was just an old man with a regrettable past, leaning on a staff in a desert by a prickly, burning bush. But God said, "I am the God of your father."

Do you remember me? God was saying, Your father believed in me. I was his God. Then He added, I am the God of Abraham, Isaac, and Jacob—the trinity of leadership in the Old Testament. And now you, Moses, He was saying. God was preparing Moses for the work ahead by reminding him of His past faithfulness to Moses' forefathers. He often prepares us in the same manner.

Did you ever think that you might be a Moses? That in the ages to come you might be the next person, in whatever job or assignment you have, to be the fulfillment of God's plan? That your regrets, however deep, may not disqualify you for pivotal service for the Lord God? His promises are not always fully realized in the present.

See the Lord in the lonely moments of your life and hear Him call you by name and say "I am your God." That's all you and I need. You do not always see the implications of your obedience to His words, nor do you always have insight into what your future will be in His eternal purpose.

Father, thank You that in an average, normal day we can see the hand of an all-powerful and an all-knowing God. In the deserts of life, You appear in the flame of Your presence. Thank You that You want us to know not only what You do, but who You are. Cause us today to remember that You are with us, watching us, ready to use us. In Jesus' name, Amen.

THE GOD WHO INTERVENES

The LORD said, "I have indeed seen the misery of my people in Egypt. I have heard them crying out because of their slave drivers, and I am concerned about their suffering. So I have come down to rescue them from the hand of the Egyptians . . . So now, go. I am sending you to Pharaoh to bring my people the Israelites out of Egypt."

But Moses said to God, "Who am I, that I should go to Pharaoh and bring the Israelites out of Egypt?"

And God said, "I will be with you. And this will be the sign to you that it is I who have sent you: When you have brought the people out of Egypt, you will worship God on this mountain."

> *Moses said to God, "Suppose I go to the Israelites and say to*
> *them, 'The God of your fathers has sent me to you,' and they ask*
> *me, 'What is his name?' Then what shall I tell them?"*
>
> *God said to Moses, "I AM WHO I AM. This is what you are*
> *to say to the Israelites: 'I AM has sent me to you.'" (Exodus 3: 7–8,*
> *10–14)*

Moses was in the afternoon of his life. Surely he thought, even standing beside the burning bush, that no adventure awaited him after all those years. At that point, because of his guilt and his past, he appeared to be stalled. Yet God called Moses to an unbelievable challenge, a seemingly impossible mission. "Rescue My people," He said. "I will be with you."

God understood Moses' fear. He also understood the Israelites' pain. Our God sees affliction and tears; He is watching the oppressor. And when we most need it, He sends help.

For Moses, as for us, many times the place of failure becomes the place of new power. It's just the reverse of the way we tend to think: that we get stronger, stronger, stronger. No.

The Bible says we go down before we go up. Jesus said, "Unless a kernel of wheat falls to the ground and dies, it remains only a single seed. But if it dies, it produces many seeds" (John 12:24). In other words, the way to resurrection is crucifixion. John the Baptist knew that, and he said of Jesus, "He must increase, but I must decrease" (John 3:30 KJV).

From a human perspective, Moses was qualified for the task before him. He knew the enemy. He had lived with them for forty years and knew exactly the way they thought. He knew their stratagems, their military, their chariots. If anybody was right for the job, it was Moses. But past disappointments intensify doubt and discouragement, so he was reluctant and asked, "Who am I?" But what mattered was not who Moses was but who God is. The same is true for us. We need to realize that our greatest usefulness comes when we are not in control of our circumstances but God is.

In spite of his qualifications, Moses felt genuinely insufficient. He didn't pretend to be confident. Moses was standing before God with bare, filthy feet, covering his eyes. He was afraid to look at God. The assignment was overwhelming.

"I see," God compassionately responded. He had brought Moses to that point to say, "I see the misery of the people. I hear their cries. I see their tears. And I know exactly what *you* are going through. I will be with you when you come out of Egypt." Not "*if* you come out of Egypt" but "*when* you come out of Egypt."

Why then did Moses say, "What if?" Because he was human. It wasn't that he didn't understand. At that point, instead of questioning God, he should have just said, "I'm ready!" But instead he asked, "Who am I?" and "What if?" He truly felt humble and insufficient.

But again, the concern should never be about who we are, but with who He is. He is God! "I will be with you. I see you where you are, and I will come to you," He said to Moses and is saying to us. Did he need anything more than that? Do we need anything more than that?

Remember the day by the Sea of Galilee recorded in John 6? The crowds gathered to listen to Jesus teach, and they grew hungry. Jesus took two fish and five loaves of bread, a small offering from a willing little boy, and he miraculously fed the whole crowd. But Jesus saw more than just their physical need for food. He saw their spiritual hunger and told them, "I am the living bread that came down from heaven" (John 6:51). And that's what God did with Moses: He came down and said, "Moses, I am with you."

God told Isaiah the prophet, "Say to those with fearful hearts, "Be strong, do not fear; your God will come" (Isa. 35:4). Isaiah urged God to "rend the heavens and come down" (64:1). God promised Isaiah and Moses, and He promises us, "He that dwelleth in the secret place of the most High shall abide under the shadow of the Almighty . . . I will be with him in trouble; I will deliver him, and honour him. With long life will I satisfy him, and shew him my salvation" (Ps. 91:1, 15–16 KJV).

Let's begin each day hearing that whisper of God in our hearts: "I AM WHO I AM."

His name is enough. It isn't "I was" or "I will be," but "I am." There is no future or past tense with God. He is the God who intervenes—today.

Father, thank You that You are with us anywhere we go, even to the end of the age. We bless You and thank You, worship

You, honor You, and love You. Help us to understand that You are the God of all the seasons of our life, that our past is covered by Your faithful forgiveness, and that our future is designed by You, the all-wise God. We want so deeply to serve You, to demonstrate to You that we are grateful that we are Your sheep and Your servants. We thank You in Jesus' name. Amen.

3

THROW DOWN YOUR ROD

Moses answered, "What if they do not believe me or listen to me and say, 'The LORD did not appear to you'?"

Then the LORD said to him, "What is that in your hand?"

"A staff," he replied

The LORD said, "Throw it on the ground."

Moses threw it on the ground and it became a snake, and he ran from it. Then the LORD said to him, "Reach out your hand and take it by the tail." So Moses reached out and took hold of the snake and it turned back into a staff in his hand. "This," said the LORD, "is so that they may believe that the LORD, the God of their fathers . . . has appeared to you." (Exodus 4:1–5)

I n spite of God's blessings upon us, we have a tendency not to trust Him completely. How God is accomplishing His plans for us is often a mystery. We don't understand and because of that, there is uncertainty. We become weak, failing to trust His promises. Of course, this is Moses' dilemma.

After forty years of being someone important (the Prince of Egypt) followed by forty years of being no one special (just a desert shepherd), Moses lingered on the back side of a desert now to learn by hard experience that God would be everything to him. He was a man alone and in a barren place. He stood right at the edge of Mount Horeb, where he would later lead the people of Israel and two hundred thousand of them would worship. He didn't know that at this point, of course; he knew only hot sand, blazing sun, and a dry throat. He had failed, and failure inevitably leads to discouragement and self-doubt.

That's where the devil keeps so many of us stuck in our weakness. He reminds us of our pasts when we ought to remind him of his future—he doesn't have one. Do you ever sense that, in your most sincere efforts to be close to God, sins, mistakes, and regrets flood your mind? They remind me how weak and insufficient I am, and this feeling is crippling. My faith fluctuates, and my personal motivation fades.

Moses' example is typical. At that point in his life, he could only see one day at a time. Even though God had promised His presence and Moses' success, Moses still asked again, "What if?"

That's the paradox of faith. We can revel in the promises of God about Christ's return and reign and about the new heaven and the new earth. We love to read the last chapters of Revelation, but we get hung up on our immediate problems. The problems of war, disease, famine, the plague of AIDS, and weapons of mass destruction blur the vision of the ultimate reign and rule of the King of Kings and the Prince of Peace. Many times, our theology about the immutable works of God crumbles in the face of "What if?"

Yet God is gracious to us—as He was to Moses. He said, "All right, I'll deal with the 'What ifs.' What do you have in your hand?" Moses said, "A staff." This was a rod about six feet long. It was a walking pole. He leaned on that staff to get a little rest, or he used it as a weapon to defend the flock he was shepherding. But the rod was more than a tool; it was also a symbol of power and authority, a sign of a person's tribe and identity. In fact, the word *rod* in the Old Testament means "tribe" in over 250 references. Every tribe had a rod.

So God told Moses, "Throw it down." Moses obeyed, and instantly the rod became a snake. It was a miracle of God and a demonstration of His power.

You have a rod in your hand, a ruling authority in your life. Are you going to keep your hand grasped tightly on it, ruling your own life, or will you throw it down in faith? Will you let God rule in—and guide—you?

Maybe you're just a cerebral or a cultural Christian. You haven't become a believer by conviction and conversion and repented of your failure and sins, asking God to forgive you and come into your life. Do you need to give your soul to God, really become a true believer in Jesus Christ, God's Son, and follow Him?

If you are trusting in Christ for your salvation and know that you are His, even in your struggles, like Moses, you can be confident that He is in control. Believe and do what God says. The life-changing consequences will be limitless, and the results will be confidence and peace of mind.

Oh God, we don't want to step ahead or step behind in Your plans for our lives. We want to say, "Lord, You be with us. You go before us." We pray that we will have the courage to throw down our rods and release the control of our lives to You as the sovereign Lord of all. We remember that Moses willingly led Your people and that Jesus willingly gave His life for all as the deliverer of those who follow Him. We now give You praise and glory in Jesus' name. Amen.

4

LOOK AHEAD

By faith Moses, when he had grown up, refused to be known as the son of Pharaoh's daughter. He chose to be mistreated along with the people of God rather than to enjoy the pleasures of sin for a short time. He regarded disgrace for the sake of Christ as of greater value than the treasures of Egypt, because he was looking ahead to his reward. By faith he left Egypt, not fearing the king's anger; he persevered because he saw him who is invisible. (Hebrews 11:24–27)

The lessons of the past become the principles for the future. In Hebrews 11, we have a chronicle of the least known and the most prominent men and women of faith. Moses is included. In spite of his previous failures and his initial reluctance to rescue God's people, he did accomplish the mission God gave him. "As also Moses was faithful in all his house, so [Christ Jesus] was counted worthy of more glory than Moses, inasmuch as he who hath builded the house hath more honour than the house . . . whose house we are, if we hold fast the confidence and the rejoicing of the hope firm unto the end" (Heb. 3:2–3, 6 KJV).

Imagine Moses' journey: He was delivered from the bulrushes, received care and comfort from Pharaoh's daughter, was treated as royalty. He spent his first four decades as a prince and the heir of Egypt. God's providence protected and prospered him. In Pharaoh's house, he could have concluded that this was his destiny, imagining that he would assume the throne, restore the people, free them from their slavery, and that Egypt could assimilate them and the pagan society could be changed to the worship of God, a true cultural revolution. But God's purposes rarely come in the form of a cultural revolution. "[God] is not willing that any should perish, but that all should come to repentance" (2 Peter 3:9 KJV). But all will not repent and the world will continue to decline; peace will be elusive until the Lord Jesus Christ returns and establishes His reign and kingdom forever.

We don't know what Moses really thought or all the things he may have done to prepare himself for God's service, but we can know that he believed God and acted in obedience in spite of negative consequences. "By faith Moses, when he had grown up, refused to be known as the son of Pharaoh's daughter. He chose to be mistreated along with the people of God . . . because he was looking ahead to his reward. By faith he left Egypt, not fearing the king's anger." In short, Moses persevered.

To persevere means to endure: to stay fixed, to hold on, to abide, to stay with it. Moses persevered because he saw Him who is invisible. He saw the culmination of his efforts and God's purposes: God's glory, God's people, God's plan, God's land, God's covenants, God's Messiah, God's reign. He knew that God's plans would be fulfilled. Isn't this the faith vision we should have?

Are you assuming that your life is always going to be

the way it is today? It isn't. There will be deserts, flames from a bush, and many other things you can't understand. All of us will experience heartache and times of uncertainty, but God says, "I AM WHO I AM" (Ex. 3:14), and Jesus is "the same yesterday and today and forever" (Heb. 13:8). Do we just sulk and feel sorry for ourselves rather than seeing that what we are going through is something God will use for His ultimate glory?

God wants us to live in faith. And what is faith? Faith comes by apprehending God's Word, accepting it personally, and applying it in your life. Paul the Apostle describes obedience as coming from faith (see Rom. 1:5). What you know to be ultimately true determines what you do. Faith is to trust what God has planned, to act decisively and deliberately. It is to persevere no matter what our circumstances.

Take Moses' life from the far side of the desert and project it forward to the Passover, the deliverance from Egypt, and his receiving the Law of God. Take your life and project it forward. Can you see God using you? Will you believe Him as He calls you to Himself and His service, or are you jeopardizing your faith? Is anything in your life deflecting from a total embracing of Jesus Christ and His plan for you? Any secret sin? Any hidden thought? Any presumption?

The ability to be holy and powerful and effective is to take that which is inevitable, that which is sure, that which is the promise of God, and bank our lives on it. Hebrews 12:1 reminds us, "Since we are surrounded by such a great cloud of witnesses"—somebody's watching us all the time: people, angels, demons, and especially the Lord—"let us throw off everything that hinders and the sin that so easily entangles, and let us run with perseverance the race marked out for us." So we should lay aside every weight and sin and look unto Jesus, the Author and Finisher of our faith. He is the one who started it, and He is the one who will complete it.

The Bible says that Moses, during a deadly plague, held up a symbolic fiery serpent on a long pole as God had instructed him to do, saying that anyone who looked to it would live (Num. 21:8). The serpent itself is a figure of sin, and brass is a symbol of judgment. The brazen serpent, set on the pole, graphically portrays sin that is judged. Christ on the cross took on Himself sin's judgment, and whoever looks to Him in faith, belives in Him, will not perish but has eternal life. Jesus said that as Moses lifted up that serpent in the wilderness, so He would be lifted up on the cross and all who looked on Him would be saved (John 3:14). The cross was a long way from the far side of the desert, but Moses looked ahead and saw it. Though he failed at times, he persevered by believing and obeying God.

No wonder Scripture says that without faith, it's impossible to please God (Heb. 11:6). Faith is the virtue that enables us to believe and obey the Word of God, for faith comes from hearing and hearing from the Word of God (Rom. 10:17).

Heavenly Father, I pray that the principles of Your Word will be written on my heart. Lord, take out of my life anything that would impede my growth, and pour continued grace into my life so that I will be faithful to live and act for You. In Jesus' name, Amen.

5

THE LAMB SLAIN FOR US

The LORD said to Moses and Aaron in Egypt, ". . . On the tenth day of this month each man is to take a lamb for his family, one for each household . . . The animals you choose must be year-old males without defect . . . Take care of them until the fourteenth day of the month, when all the people of the community of Israel must slaughter them at twilight. Then they are to take some of the blood and put it on the sides and tops of the doorframes of the houses where they eat the lambs. That same night they are to eat the meat roasted over the fire, along with bitter herbs, and bread made without yeast . . . Eat it in haste; it is the LORD's Passover.

"On that same night I will pass through Egypt and strike down every firstborn—both men and animals—and I will bring judgment on all the gods of Egypt. I am the LORD. The blood will be a sign for you on the houses where you are; and when I see the blood, I will pass over you . . . Take none of the meat outside the house. Do not break any of the bones."
(Exodus 12:1, 3, 5–8, 11–13, 46)

Finally, Moses said to Pharaoh: "This is the word of the Lord. This is from the God who delivers. This is what the Lord, who is God, said: every firstborn—even that of the man on the throne, the man in prison, the slave, and all animals—in this nation will die."

Pharaoh heard the warning, but he strongly resisted and his heart was hardened. So Moses instructed the people; they all sacrificed lambs, smeared the blood over the doorframes, and roasted the meat for the meal. All night long, they heard the wail of Egypt mourning the deaths of all its firstborn. This was the night of the Passover.

Pharaoh called Moses and Aaron and said, "Take your

people and leave at once. If you don't go, we all will die." The fear of God and of His judgment had fallen on the nation of Egypt.

Throughout Scripture miraculous events changed all of Israel and foreshadowed everything in history until the incarnation of the Lord Jesus. When the disciple John saw Jesus, he said, "Look, *the* Lamb of God, who takes away the sin of the world!" (John 1:29, emphasis added). At that point, the lamb of the Passover finds its ultimate fulfillment in the person of Jesus Christ. The first sacrifice recorded in the Bible was Abel offering a lamb for himself, the sins of one man. In the Passover, it was a lamb for the sins of all who were in a household. In the crucifixion of Christ on the cross, it is a lamb for the sins of the whole world.

When the Israelites slew lambs, they were lambs for the family or the household. When the Lord God presented His Lamb, He was the Lamb for me, a sinner, and you, too. Jesus said, "I have come to give my life as a ransom for many" (Matt. 20:28).

Isaiah wrote that the crucifixion was the work of God: "It pleased the LORD to bruise him; he hath put him to grief" for our iniquities (Isa. 53:10 KJV). God made His Son an offering for sin. Christ the Lamb bore punishment, ignominy, injustice, and injury.

Every punch and stinging slap Jesus suffered was the result of my sins. The Roman soldiers put a stick in His hand, a symbolic scepter, and mocked Him as a king. They whipped Him, making lacerations by a jagged tearing of the flesh, on His back. They put a crown of thorns on His head—long ones, not like the little barbs on a rosebush. They pushed the ready-made crown down into the skin of His head, perforating His scalp. And as the blood spurted out, they screamed, "Hail, King!"

Then they crucified Him. Oh, what a phrase! "And sitting down they watched him there" (Matt. 27: 36 KJV). Thank the Lord we don't have too many details—His appearance was disfigured beyond that of any man (Isa. 52:14). They drove nails into His flesh and hung Him by His pierced hands. Just as the Israelites were not to break the bones of the Passover lamb, no one fractured Jesus' bones either. John, who was there, recorded the scene: "When they came to Jesus and found that he was already dead, they did not break his legs. Instead, one of the soldiers pierced Jesus' side with a spear, bringing a sudden flow of blood and water" (John 19:33–34). The pericardial sac was punctured.

So with Jesus there was the bruising, the laceration, the perforation, the incision, and the penetration. The five wounds of Jesus were wounds of betrayal and hatred and malice, wounds of judgment but also wounds of love. His wounds forgive; His wounds heal; His wounds restore.

Our sins are paid for by the blood of Christ, but in order for the Lamb's work to be effective in our lives, we must receive Him as our Savior and glorify Him (John 1:12). Until we get beyond the historic Jesus of Nazareth, we really don't understand why He died. Until then, He is just a teacher or a prophet, perhaps one of many. But when we see Jesus the Christ, the Lamb of God, with our hearts opened in faith, God reveals His Son sent from heaven to save us.

The word *savior* appears only twenty-four times in all of the New Testament. But the word *lord* appears more than nine hundred times: "God has made this Jesus, whom you crucified, both Lord and Christ" (Acts 2:36). No wonder Paul wrote, "For we do not preach ourselves, but Jesus Christ as Lord" (2 Cor. 4:5). Now by the resurrection as Lord, the emphasis of Scripture intensifies as to who He is, Lord of life and death. Naturally then "Christ shall be magnified in my body, whether it be by life, or by death. For to me to live is Christ, and to die is gain" (Phil. 1:20–21 KJV). And that's what your confession should be: "I will magnify the lamb who was slain, who is now Lord and Christ." *Magnify* means to make something increase. John says, "He must increase, but I must decrease" (John 3:30 KJV). Should we not exalt Him since His name is above every other name? His name is power and deliverance and hope to all who love Him.

Do you know the Lamb? Have you been made clean by the blood of the One who was put to death as your sacrifice? And why was the Lamb slain? "For God so loved the world that he gave his one and only Son that whoever believes in him shall not perish but have eternal life" (John 3:16). Have you believed in Jesus, saying, "Yes, I want the Lamb's blood to cover me; I want judgment and hell to pass over and spare me"? Each of us can then say, I have trusted in the Lamb. I worship the Lamb. And someday I will reign with the Lamb because my name is written in the Lamb's Book of Life (Rev. 21:23–27).

Father, we thank You and bless You for Your Son, the Lamb of God, and for His glorious victory over death and hell. There is nothing that we can offer other than our hearts in loving gratitude for the unsearchable riches of Your grace. For the sinless Lamb, Your Son, who poured out His precious blood for our sins, we say hallelujah and pray that our hearts will be transformed by your great love and sacrifice. And it is all to Your glory. In Jesus' name, Amen.

PART II

DISCIPLESHIP:

THE

BASICS

6

FORGIVENESS: PASS IT ON

Do not grieve the Holy Spirit of God, with whom you were sealed for the day of redemption. Get rid of all bitterness, rage and anger, brawling and slander, along with every form of malice. Be kind and compassionate to one another, forgiving each other, just as in Christ God forgave you. Be imitators of God, therefore, as dearly loved children and live a life of love, just as Christ loved us and gave himself up for us as a fragrant offering and sacrifice to God. (Ephesians 4:30—5:2)

In the Lord's Prayer, we say, "Forgive us for our faults. Forgive us for the things we've done to You as we forgive those who did the same to us: offended, slandered, criticized, betrayed us, and hurt our feelings."

But is it that simple? Can we forgive as easily as we receive forgiveness? God's pardon is so accessible. When we say, "God, forgive me," we know He does. We know our confession leads to purity: David wrote, "I acknowledged my sin to you and did not cover up my iniquity . . . and you forgave the guilt of my sin" (Ps. 32:5). With God, forgiveness and restoration are readily available and waiting for us.

And what is the basis of that forgiveness? How can such a righteous God "forget about" our sinfulness? The answer is Jesus! Romans 3:24 says we "are justified freely by his grace through the redemption that came by Christ Jesus." God sent Jesus, and Jesus wore the guilt of our sins. Peter wrote, "He himself bore our sins in his body on the tree . . . by his wounds you have been healed [or forgiven of sins]" (1 Peter 2:24). God did everything necessary to provide for our forgiveness by sacrificing His perfect, holy Son as the atoning substitute for our sins.

With such a sufficient provision as Christ, the forgiveness of God is profound, reaching far beyond any concept we have of it. When He forgives, He cancels our debt. He releases us from the eternal consequences of our sin. He tears up our IOUs. The pardon of God deletes past, present, and future sins—completely!

The Bible uses the word "forgiveness" six hundred times; it means "to lift off, to relieve, to cleanse, and to cancel a debt." When you have forgiveness, you have freedom. That's why on the cross Jesus said, "It is finished" (John 19:30).

So forgiveness from God to us is free and complete. But when we have to extend forgiveness to each other, we often feel grossly incapable. Why is it so hard for us to forgive? Because, although it is God's nature to love and to forgive, we don't have a nature like that—we want to get even. Romans 7:18 puts it succinctly: "I know that in me (that is, in my flesh,) dwelleth no good thing" (KJV). Also, the depth of our hurt creates the length of our inability to forgive. And we don't want to forget. It seems too easy to let people off the hook. We don't forgive because we're afraid we're going to be hurt again.

Yet God has not given us an option. Paul wrote that the forgiveness we have received is something we must pass along: "Be kind and compassionate to one another, forgiving each other, just as in Christ God forgave you" (Eph. 4:32). He reminds us that if we don't forgive others, we give the devil an advantage (2 Cor. 2:10–11). Satan can't stop forgiveness from the throne to the sinner, but he can hinder forgiveness from one believer to another.

We Christians should remember that we are abundantly forgiven and let that inspire us to forgive others. When people break a relationship and make up again, they do so only at the expense of the cross. Forgiveness and reconciliation are gifts from God that we extend to others. They originate with Him, with the Cross, and overflow to others. In Christ, God was reconciling the world to Himself and committing to us the ministry of reconciliation (2 Cor. 5:18–19): bringing people to Himself, participating in His redemptive forgiveness.

Remember that with God, forgiveness is forever. In heaven, His forgiveness will still be in place. That's why the pardoned person will never be lost. God loves, He forgives,

He saves, He sanctifies, He glorifies with the same essence of His eternal self. He will never change, so neither will His forgiveness. He has promised that His own are "kept by the power of God through faith unto salvation" (1 Peter 1:5 KJV).

Our forgiveness toward others should flow from a realization and appreciation of God's forgiveness toward us. So let us be kind one to another, compassionate, living in love and forgiving one another, even as God forgave us because of Jesus Christ.

How we thank You, O Lord Jesus, that we live without obligation other than love. We live without debt, because You paid it by Your precious blood. You, the Lamb who was slain, are living today, the highest King. We bless You. Lord, where there is any feeling of hurt that we will not release, any relationship trouble that we could solve, help us to do that. Forgive us our trespasses. You have forgiven us; help us to have a forgiving spirit and not hold grudges or become bitter because others have offended us. Help us to forgive them in the reconciliation of the Cross. In His name, Amen.

7

Sin's Remedy

If you think you are standing firm, be careful that you don't fall! No temptation has seized you except what is common to man. And God is faithful; he will not let you be tempted beyond what you can bear. But when you are tempted, he will also provide a way out so that you can stand up under it. (1 Corinthians 10:12—13)

Because he himself suffered when he was tempted, he is able to help those who are being tempted . . . We do not have a high priest who is unable to sympathize with our weaknesses, but we have one who has been tempted in every way, just as we are—

yet was without sin. Let us then approach the throne of grace
with confidence, so that we may receive mercy and find grace to
help us in our time of need. (Hebrews 2:18, 4:15—16)

D o you ever feel alone in temptations—that you are
the only one having to suffer such harsh battles of
the spirit? Paul wrote in 1 Corinthians 10 that no temptation is unique to one person; every invitation to sin is common among mankind. Don't feel singled out. The devil will
try each one of us as he even tried Christ! Christ was
tempted in all points yet lived without sinning. He knows
what we are going through, and He will strengthen us.

In life, we face both *temptations* and *trials.* Trials are testings—the difficult circumstances, painful events, and surprise setbacks that plague us all. Temptations are the actual
enticements of the devil to sin against God and each other.
We give in to temptation when we disregard any of God's
commandments.

Sometimes we think testings and temptations come in
life because we're backslidden people or because we need to

learn a lesson. Not so. We can be tempted and tested when we're full of the Spirit. In fact, many times the greatest temptations confront us when we are in the center of the will of God, because being there has offset and frustrated Satan's methods of attack.

The devil is a powerful, cosmic, and wicked being. The Book of Job says he has a globetrotting ability: "going to and fro in the earth, and . . . walking up and down in it" (1:7 KJV). He "masquerades as an angel of light," Paul wrote (2 Cor. 11:14). And the Bible says he's at the throne of God right now, every day, day and night, accusing the brethren (Rev. 12:10).

As relentless as our enemy's challenges can be, Paul also wrote to the Corinthians that God has not left us alone to cope with them. Neither trials nor temptations will be so extreme that we will not have the ability to endure them. He will not allow you to be pressured or put to any test beyond what you "are able to cope with," and He will also "make a way to escape" (1 Cor. 10:13 KJV). God is reliable. He will be there, whatever the devil uses against you. God will allow difficult circumstances to go only so far, and then He'll reach in and bring you through.

What are the ways of escape that God provides? We can read the Word of God: "Thy word have I hid in mine heart, that I might not sin against thee" (Ps. 119:11 KJV). We can pray: "Watch and pray so you will not fall into temptation" (Matt. 26:41). And we can depend on God's deliverance: "I will be with him in trouble, I will deliver him and honor him" (Ps. 91:15).

When we are weak in temptation, we have to realize that we have, as it says in the Scripture, access to Him: "Let us then approach the throne of grace with confidence, so that we may receive mercy and find grace to help us in our time of need" (Heb. 4:16). His grace saves, His grace satisfies, and His grace sustains us in difficulty.

The New Testament writers remind us that God is "rich in mercy" (Eph. 2:4), "faithful" (1 Cor. 10:13), and that He will "supply all your need according to his riches in glory by Christ Jesus" (Phil. 4:19 KJV). The word "supply" means to bring to the top. Therefore the verse might read, "My God shall have capacity to meet all your needs."

The word "riches" means resources. "Riches" is the strongest word we can use. No word fully explains the abundance of God's resources and the fullness of His mercy. When we talk about the riches of His grace, we are defining the exhaustless characteristic of God, because His grace can never be used up. It can never be drained. When God supplies, there is never any depletion of His resources because His riches are without limit. The grace capacity of God is something we can never exhaust.

God's everlasting attributes are part of the solution to our temptation to sin; His Son is another. Jesus, as we've mentioned, knows exactly how biting temptation can be. The writer of Hebrews recorded that "he himself suffered" in temptation and endured, and therefore can empathize with and empower us when we are under attack. Our High Priest Jesus yet lives to minister to us, to save us not only from sin's eternal consequences but to enable us to withstand temptation's push and pull. He alone has confronted and defeated the devil and never sinned (Heb. 4:15; 1 Peter 2:22). Call on Him when you feel weak and vulnerable.

When temptation overcomes us—and it will at times—our High Priest also forgives us. "He is able also to save them to the uttermost that come unto God by him, seeing he [always] liveth to make intercession for them" (Heb. 7:25 KJV). "He shall save his people from their sins" (Matt. 1:21 KJV). "He is the atoning sacrifice for our sins, and not only for ours but also for the sins of the whole world" (1 John 2:2). Therefore we have both help to endure temptation and pardon when we fall into it—we have every remedy for sin. We have Jesus.

Father, You told us in Your Word that You, who are rich in mercy, will provide a way of escape when sin entices us. You are our Advocate and defend us when accused by the enemy of our souls. Give us courage to believe that. Trials and testings will come, but You are faithful and will not allow us to be tempted above that which we are able to handle. We thank You for Your rescue and for Jesus. You, Lord, shall supply all our needs according to Your riches in glory through Christ Jesus. We pray in His name, Amen.

8

FOLLOW ME

*He calls his own sheep by name and leads them out. When he
has brought out all his own, he goes on ahead of them . . . I am
the good shepherd . . . My sheep listen to my voice; I know
them, and they follow me.*

*Whoever serves me must follow me; and where I am, my
servant also will be. (John 10:3–4, 14, 27, 12:26)*

When the word "follow" appears in the New
Testament, it implies being a companion, someone who goes along in the same way as another person. The

ancient Greek world had the idea of the peripatetic school, in which one stayed with his teacher at all times; you lived in the same house with him. The student wrote down what the teacher said, reacted to the teacher's questions, and watched how the teacher did what he did. The student studied the integrity of the teacher, his lifestyle, and learned to follow him and replicate him. Early believers were called "the followers of Christ," those who were companions and students of Jesus.

As Christians, we are to live by this peripatetic model, this pattern of following the Lord Jesus as His companions, His students. Jesus is our pattern: What He did, we do. Christ left us "an example, that [we] should follow in his steps" (1 Peter 2:21). "I have set you an example that you should do as I have done," Jesus said (John 13:15). Paul wrote, "Follow my example, as I follow the example of Christ" (1 Cor. 11:1). We may want to be leaders, but the Lord requires of us to be followers, because He is our Shepherd and we are His sheep.

A follower is never greater than his leader; a follower never draws attention to himself. When the disciples said to Jesus, "We have cast out demons," they were doing what their leader had given them power to do. But wasn't it a point of pride that the demons were subject to them? The process and the power of exorcism seduced them to forget that their authority was not in themselves or in their ability to perform this miracle but in the name of Jesus, to whom all the demons are subject. Jesus scolded them and reminded them that Satan had fallen from heaven because of his desire to take power for himself. "I have given you authority," He said, ". . . to overcome all the power of the enemy; nothing will harm you. However, do not rejoice that the spirits submit to you, but rejoice that your names are written in heaven" (Luke 10:19–20).

We have to be careful that anything we undertake in the name of Jesus Christ we do for one ultimate purpose: His glory, not ours. We can't focus on our personal performance or on the performance of our ministries—it is common to think that activity in the service of Christ is the indication of the blessing of God but be aware of barrenness in a busy life. There is an over-emphasis on performance in public ministry to the detriment of the Gospel and the holy character of Jesus our Lord. We are carriers of the gospel, not entertainers in the display of our talents. Both are gifts of Jesus, through the Holy Spirit. "Blessed are the pure in heart," Jesus said, "for they will see God" (Matt. 5:8). Our actions are seen by people, but our motives are monitored by God.

"The fruit of the Spirit is love, joy, peace, patience, kindness, goodness, faithfulness, gentleness and self-control" (Gal. 5:22–23). When a person exhibits the fruit of the Spirit in his life, it is the evidence of the life of Jesus. Jesus pictured this in horticultural terms. A good tree gives good fruit. Fruit is the product of a living organism, and the quality and character of the fruit is determined by the quality and character of the tree. Since the godly person is compared to a tree planted by water that produces fruit seasonally; we, as followers of Christ, should be producing the likeness of Christ every day. Jesus said that when this takes place, people will see our good works and "glorify [our] Father which is in heaven" (Matt. 5:16 KJV).

Another aspect of following is to pursue or to keep it up continuously. The apostle Paul told us, "O man of God . . . follow after righteousness, godliness, faith, love, patience, meekness. Fight the good fight of faith, lay hold on eternal life" (1 Tim. 6:11–12 KJV). We pursue righteousness when we flee the things that keep us from following the Lord Jesus. These are the keys: flee, follow, and fight. What do you need to do in order to pursue righteousness?

We're told to "throw off everything that hinders and the sin that so easily entangles, and let us run with perseverance" (Heb. 12:1). The heart is what God wants: tender, humble, clean, surrendered. Our passion should be, "Create in me a clean heart, O God; and renew a right spirit within me" (Ps. 51:10 KJV).

Jesus, the Good Shepherd, said, "When he has brought out all his own, he goes on ahead of them, and his sheep follow him because they know his voice . . . I have come that they may have life, and have it to the full" (John 10:4, 10).

Father, may our lives reflect that we're not only believers but also followers. As Your followers, we pray that we will always hear Your voice and that You will lead us as our Great Shepherd. We thank You again for the unchanging relationship we have with You as our Shepherd and that we have eternal life because You have laid down Your life for us as Your sheep. In Jesus' name, Amen.

9

KEYS TO WORSHIP

Give thanks to the LORD, call on his name;

make known among the nations what he has done.

Sing to him, sing praise to him;

tell of all his wonderful acts.

Glory in his holy name;

let the hearts of those who seek the LORD rejoice.

Look to the LORD and his strength;

seek his face always.

Remember the wonders he has done,

his miracles, and the judgments he pronounced.

O descendants of Israel his servant,

O sons of Jacob, his chosen ones.

He is the LORD our God;

his judgments are in all the earth.

He remembers his covenant forever,

the word he commanded, for a thousand generations . . .

When [the people of Israel] were but few in number,

few indeed, and strangers in it,

they wandered from nation to nation,

from one kingdom to another.

He allowed no man to oppress them;

For their sake he rebuked kings . . .

Sing to the LORD, all the earth;

proclaim his salvation day after day.

Declare his glory among the nations,

his marvelous deeds among all peoples.

For great is the LORD and most worthy of praise;

he is to be feared above all gods.

For all the gods of the nations are idols,

but the LORD made the heavens.

Splendor and majesty are before him;

strength and joy in his dwelling place.

Ascribe to the LORD, O families of nations,
ascribe to the LORD glory and strength,
ascribe to the LORD the glory due his name . . .
Let the heavens rejoice, let the earth be glad;
let them say among the nations, "The LORD reigns!" . . .
Give thanks to the LORD, for he is good;
his love endures forever . . .
Praise be to the LORD, the God of Israel,
from everlasting to everlasting.
(1 Chronicles 16:8—15, 19—21, 23—29, 31, 34, 36)

Think about the word *worship*. The expression of worship can become controversial when we discuss musical style, the use of instruments, congregational participation, and questioning what is appropriate and effective. How can worship become more relevant to human needs? Conferences and publications center on the subject of worship and its changes. Also, there is an explosion in the marketing and promotion of praise and worship music. Worship continues to be a common but important subject.

But sometimes words that are common become pale by overexposure. We use them so frequently that their real meanings don't quite affect us as they should.

Worshiping God begins by recognizing who God is, His attributes, and how God expresses Himself in His works. Telling God we know how good and powerful He is makes worship outwardly expressive. In the passage from I Chronicles, David praised God not simply to himself but outwardly, saying, "You reprove kings on our behalf. You are great and worthy. You are the Creator. You are splendor and majesty. Glory, honor, strength, and gladness are all Your properties. You are a king; You rule. You are worthy of gratitude, and we need to give You thanks. You are a good God, a merciful God, a saving God. You deliver, and You are our God. You are the Lord God of Israel."

Worship is just that simple. When we seek to express worship to God, four attitudes shape our approach to Him. The first is *reverence*. Psalm 8:3–4 says, "When I consider your heavens, / the work of your fingers . . . / what is man that you are mindful of him?" Worship always begins by acknowledging God as supreme. Our Creator is an all-surpassing God.

He supersedes everything and everyone. Because He is so high and lofty, I am humbled and reverence Him. I yield. I submit because He is greater, wiser, and Lord above all.

When we revere someone, we realize we are "less than" that person. What did the wise men do at the manger? Before they gave the presents to Jesus and His family, they worshiped Him. They knew who He was, and they bowed down before the child Jesus, whom they venerated as King. When the Lord Jesus comes again as He promised (John 14:3), like the wise men, every knee will be forced to bow and every tongue will confess that He is Lord, to the glory of God (Phil. 2:10–11). So the essence of worship is reverence.

Second, worship is *spiritual*. Those who worship the Lord must do so "in spirit and in truth," Jesus said (John 4:24). By "spirit" Jesus meant that our worship must be more than just outward expression, it must also take place in our spirits. Gestures can be the outward expressions of worship, but it is the attitude of the heart that God sees. The Biblical term is "the heart." We worship in our hearts—it is a spiritual matter. Its center is our whole inner being.

Also, the location of worship can be very meaningful.

In each of the places that Abraham worshiped, he built an altar. So did Noah, when he came out of the ark. Joshua, when he told the people to cross the Jordan, said to take a stone for every tribe and use them to build a memorial on the other side (Josh. 4:1–9). Jesus had special locations for private prayer, the most memorable being the garden of the olive trees. Each of us needs a place of worship, such as our church. We need a place we can be reminded of God's word and reverence His presence. Primarily, though, we worship in spirit, in the sanctuary of the heart.

The third attitude is one of *veneration*. When we venerate someone, we exalt that person or being. We extol him, or her, always first in our lives. "You shall have no other gods before me" (Ex. 20:3). All other gods are not gods. Can they speak? Can they hear? Can they touch? Can they feel? Absolutely not! They're made by the hands of men. The God of Scripture is almighty, invisible, and everlasting.

The one and only true God is unique and functions independently from everything else in the universe. Truly recognizing God's supremacy will inspire us to worship Him. Peter expressed this kind of worship to Jesus when he said, "To whom shall we go? You have the words of eternal life. We believe and know that you are the Holy One of God" (John 6:68–69). Worship is veneration.

The fourth attitude is *praise,* which means to determine and acknowledge the value or worth of something. When we worship God by praising Him, we describe Him. "He's an awesome God." "He's our rock. He's our fortress. He's our deliverer." "Lord, you're so great. You're so wonderful." Words are important when we praise the Lord for this reason. They give expression for our worship (Heb. 13:15).

Worship is wonder, love, and praise. Not only does it cause us to contemplate and appreciate our holy God, but it gives us vitality, vigor, and a desire to obey Him. As the old hymn says, "Were the whole realm of nature mine, that were a present far too small; Love so amazing, so divine, demands my soul, my life, my all."[1]

Think of RSVP: reverence, spiritual, veneration, praise. In worship, we testify to God's transcendent glory. Let all the Lord's people declare that He is the one and only Lord, and there is none like Him. He is worthy to be praised.

O Lord, worthy is our wonderful God. We praise You, we exalt You. We venerate You. We reverence You. You've opened up our hearts and given us the capacity not only to know You but to love You. We humbly bow our hearts before You and stand in awe before You to serve You as our Lord. In the worthy name of Your Son, Jesus, Amen.

10

Learning to Obey

This is how the birth of Jesus Christ came about: His mother Mary was pledged to be married to Joseph, but before they came together, she was found to be with child through the Holy Spirit. Because Joseph her husband was a righteous man and did not want to expose her to public disgrace, he had in mind to divorce her quietly.

But after he had considered this, an angel of the Lord appeared to him in a dream and said, "Joseph son of David, do not be afraid to take Mary home as your wife, because what is conceived in her is from the Holy Spirit. She will give birth to a son, and you are to give him the name Jesus, because he will save his people from their sins."

All this took place to fulfill what the Lord had said through the prophet: "The virgin will be with child and will give birth to a son, and they will call him Immanuel"—which means, "God with us."

When Joseph woke up, he did what the angel of the Lord had commanded him and took Mary home as his wife . . . She gave birth to a son. And he gave him the name Jesus. (Matthew 1:18–25)

The Lord appeared to Joseph in a dream. "Get up," he said, "take the child and his mother and escape to Egypt. Stay there until I tell you, for Herod is going to search for the child to kill him."

So he got up, took the child and his mother during the night and left for Egypt, where he stayed until the death of Herod . . .

After Herod died, an angel of the Lord appeared in a dream to Joseph in Egypt and said, "Get up, take the child and his mother and go to the land of Israel, for those who were trying to take the child's life are dead." (Matthew 2:13–15, 19–20)

At Christmas, we contemplate the mystery of the angelic message and the lives of the virgin Mary, the Magi, the shepherds, and others such as Simeon and Anna. But we so often overlook Joseph, who in the nativity story is overshadowed by the blessed Virgin and seems to have a lesser role as simply the foster father of the child Jesus.

The Bible says he was a "righteous," or just, man. Paul used this word in Romans 1:17, saying, "The righteous will live by faith." To be righteous means to be a believing person, a trustful person. What we are is always noticed by God, who honors faith. Look at the way Joseph responded to God.

To Joseph's total surprise, his betrothed, Mary, was pregnant. We wonder, *What did Mary say to Joseph? How did she explain that?* Providentially, Joseph was very sensitive. He didn't want to divorce her or expose her. So whom did Joseph consult about his situation? Who was his friend? Who was his rabbi? Did he discuss this surprise pregnancy with anyone? Apparently not, he was all alone. Sometimes the deepest decisions of our lives will be made just within ourselves, especially when we have no one to turn to. God knew He could trust Joseph, and He gave him this enormous responsibility. God saw his heart of faith and obedience.

God also gave Joseph all the answers he needed. Joseph heard the message and did what the angel said in his dream. When he awoke, he protected Mary and obeyed the Lord. Isn't that love? In your marriage, don't ever do anything that would create suspicion, anxiety, anger, or alienation. Protect your spouse. Shield each other with love. Be nurturing, loving, and caring. Joseph did these things and more not only as a husband, but also as a parent for God's son.

So Joseph married Mary; she delivered a son, and Joseph named Him Jesus. By chapter 2 of Matthew's gospel, the child is a toddler, somewhere close to the age of two. When Herod found out that this "prince" was born—Herod the ruthless, local King—he issued an edict that all the children under the age of two were to be slaughtered. This event is called the Slaughter of the Innocents. Imagine how terrible it must have been to have soldiers suddenly burst into your house and murder your child.

Again God guided Joseph, "Go down to Egypt." Egypt? Joseph knew about the history of his people and why they left Egypt—they had been slaves there for over 140 years. Millions of Israelites were imprisoned as slaves in Egypt.

This was a terrifying destination. But again, he trusted God's Word and obeyed.

Joseph not only obeyed, he obeyed right away. Scripture tells us that Joseph got up in the middle of the night. He did not take time to plan out the journey or think things through. He acted immediately on what he was told. He had the whole trip to think about these sudden changes in his life. As the lonely trio started from Bethlehem they must have wondered what life's future held. How long would they be in Egypt? How would they survive? Could Joseph find work? Where would they live? How would they take care of their young son? They didn't have answers to these pressing and weighty concerns. Nevertheless, Joseph did immediately and exactly as the Lord instructed in his dream. Imagine the faith this required. When God leads us, He doesn't always tell us the long-term implications. He leads us day by day.

When Herod finally died, the angel of the Lord appeared to Joseph again in a dream. Joseph had to trust his dreams. We like to find guidance in clear Bible verses with life applications spelled out in the footnotes. But Joseph heard in a dream, "Arise, and take the young child and his mother, and go into the land of Israel: for they are dead which sought the young child's life" (Matt. 2:20 KJV). So Joseph packed up his family once again and headed, naturally, for Bethlehem. But again in a dream, God told him to go to Nazareth, which he did. Joseph was spiritually minded, sensitive to the Lord's leading, and selfless. He believed God and obeyed Him. We all need to be like that today.

A wonderful thing happens in the Christian life when we are willing to say, "Lord, what do You want me to do? How do You want me to do it? I trust You, Lord." God doesn't always tell us the whole plan, but He expects our obedience. Like Joseph, we can, by faith, fulfill His purpose by responding to His Word and learning to obey.

Heavenly Father, lead me. Help me to please You and honor You. I look to Your Word to know You and the way You will guide my life. I pray that I will be led in the beauty of Your holiness and by the guidance of Your Spirit so that I will grow in grace and in the knowledge of Your Son, the Lord Jesus Christ. I pray that I will do exactly what You expect me to do, trusting You, just as Joseph did. In Jesus' name, Amen.

PART III

DISCIPLESHIP:

BEYOND THE

BASICS

CURE FOR THE THREE DS:
DEPRESSION, DISOBEDIENCE,
DISAPPOINTMENT

*Mary stood outside the tomb crying. As she wept, she bent over
to look into the tomb . . . She turned around and saw Jesus
standing there, but she did not realize that it was Jesus . . .*

*[Jesus] said, "[Mary], why are you crying? Who is it you
are looking for?" . . .*

She turned toward him and cried out . . . ["Master!"]

*Jesus said, "Do not hold on to me, for I have not yet
returned to the Father. Go instead to my brothers and tell them,*

'I am returning to my Father and your Father, to my God and your God.'"

Mary of Magdala went to the disciples with the news: "I have seen the Lord!" And she told them that he had said these things to her. (John 20:11, 14–18)

Early in the morning, Jesus stood on the shore, but the disciples did not realize that it was Jesus. He called out to them, "Friends, haven't you any fish?" . . .

Then the disciple whom Jesus loved said to Peter, "It is the Lord!" As soon as Simon Peter heard him say, "It is the Lord," he wrapped his outer garment around him (for he had taken it off) and jumped into the water. . . .

When they had finished eating, Jesus said to Simon Peter, "Simon son of John, do you truly love me more than these?"

"Yes, Lord," he said, "you know that I love you."

Jesus said, "Feed my lambs . . . Take care of my sheep . . . Feed my sheep." (John 21:4–5, 7, 15–17)

Now that same day two of them were going to a village called Emmaus . . . Jesus himself came up and walked along with *them; but they were kept from recognizing him.*

He asked them, "What are you discussing together as you walk along?"

They stood still, their faces downcast. One of them, named Cleopas, asked him, "Are you only a visitor to Jerusalem and do not know the things that have happened there in these days?"

"What things?" he asked.

"About Jesus of Nazareth," they replied. "He was a prophet, powerful in word and deed before God and all the people. The chief priests and our rulers handed him over to be sentenced to death, and they crucified him; but we had hoped that he was the one who was going to redeem Israel" . . .

When he was at the table with them, he took bread, gave thanks, broke it and began to give it to them. Then their eyes were opened and they recognized him. (Luke 24:13, 15—21, 30—31)

J esus rose from the dead and asked three probing questions that led to three unique emotional and spiritual insights. All of these disciples were struggling and hurting, but each had now witnessed the Resurrection and could see the risen Lord as never before. Each had a specific need that required a specific solution: the Lord Himself.

First, there was Mary Magdalene, whom Jesus had delivered from seven demons. Try to imagine how she felt. Jesus was dead, or at least so she thought. She was thoroughly discouraged, emotionally unraveled. She sobbed convulsively. As her sandals flapped along the dusty little path to Jesus' tomb, she relived what she had experienced. She remembered the Lord at the time of her conversion, the love He showed her, and perhaps the last time she was close to Him.

Mary had completely relied upon Christ, the visible Jesus, the personal Christ. She was a close follower of Jesus, and she loved Him. But now, her experiences with Christ were memories, and she became totally broken. She had entered *depression,* feeling overwhelmed, as if there was no hope. Depression is a terrible, crippling feeling.

What changed Mary's life, what stopped the smothering sorrow, was that suddenly she realized He was alive. He was there in front of her. Her experience with the risen Lord was no longer past tense but present realization. Her depression dissolved in the confidence of His presence.

Peter had his own unique emotional need after Jesus was crucified. As Jesus anticipated the hour of His betrayal, He asked Peter, as well as the two sons of Zebedee, to "keep alert" with Him. As Jesus waited, He lamented, "My soul is overwhelmed with sorrow to the point of death" (Matt. 26:38). If ever He needed support from His disciples, it was then. Yet not once but three times, Peter and the other disciples fell asleep while Jesus spent those agonizing hours alone.

Peter had promised Jesus, "Even if I have to die with you, I will never disown you" (Matt. 26:35). But he did just that again, not once but three times, never realizing that good intentions are often offset by fear and self-interest. Any betrayal is devastating because it is based on a relationship, often an intimate one. Those closest to you can hurt you the most.

Again, the Lord proved Himself the Redeemer. When John spotted Jesus on shore after His resurrection, Peter jumped ship to meet Him. He wanted to make things right because he realized that the Lord was there. Is there anything in our lives that we need to make right with Jesus? Will we run to meet Him as Peter did?

As the disciples shared a fish breakfast with Jesus, our Lord asked Peter pointed questions about his once-questionable commitment. Peter answered each as best he could, "You know I love You, Lord." And Jesus then assigned him tasks in what would become the pastor's role—to feed and care for Jesus' followers. He resolved Peter's *disobedience* by forgiving his failure and reinstating him to service.

And finally, there were the emotional depths of *disappointment*. Two disciples traveling to Emmaus told Jesus, whom they didn't recognize, that they "had hoped that he was the one who was going to redeem Israel" (Luke 24:21). They had longed for Him to be something other than what He apparently was. When Jesus' death had signaled the end of their dream of deliverance, His friends tumbled into disappointment and disillusionment.

Yet again, Jesus' presence melted away the emotional pain the men were feeling. When they realized that Jesus was alive and their redemption *was* at hand, it changed their disappointment to excitement. Lost hope was, and is, restored by the resurrected Lord.

It is true of every stinging experience of our lives: Jesus, and Jesus alone, can rescue us. Each of us has known discouragement if not depression, has been disobedient and has felt crushing disappointment. There is not a single thing that He cannot change, control, and conquer because He is the living Lord. Like His followers before us, we can let His presence cure us of these three Ds. Let the Lord come into your heart right now.

Oh, God, could I feel Your presence? If I'm depressed, bring me joy. If I'm disobedient, repentance. If I am discouraged, renewal. If I'm disappointed, bring me hope. I want You to restore me. I accept You as Lord of my life. Come to me personally, Lord. May I then be ready to glorify You. In Jesus' name, Amen.

12

DEALING WITH DISTRACTION

I have worked much harder, been in prison more frequently, been flogged more severely, and been exposed to death again and again. Five times I received from the Jews the forty lashes minus one. Three times I was beaten with rods, once I was stoned, three times I was shipwrecked, I spent a night and a day in the open sea, I have been constantly on the move. I have been in danger from rivers, in danger from bandits, in danger from my own countrymen, in danger from Gentiles; in danger in the city, in danger in the country, in danger at sea; and in danger from false brothers. I have labored and toiled and have often gone without sleep; I have known hunger and thirst and have

often gone without food; I have been cold and naked. Besides
everything else, I face daily the pressure of my concern for all
the churches. (2 Corinthians 11:23–28)

P aul was a man who knew distractions, considering the challenges of ministry, the opposition of his former friends, the vigorous attacks from religious leaders, natural disasters, personal weakness, deprivations, and beatings (2 Cor. 11:23–27). Only His Lord endured more.

However, nothing stopped him, at least not for long. Paul told the Ephesian leaders, "I consider my life worth nothing to me, if only I may finish the race and complete the task the Lord Jesus has given me" (Acts 20:24). In other words, Paul was saying, "I want you to know that none of these things that have bothered me are going to limit the gospel. I won't be turned aside from my mission." Even in prison he could say, "I can do all things through Christ who strengthens me" (Phil. 4:13); "I count all things but loss for the excellency of the knowledge of Christ Jesus my Lord" (Phil. 3:8 KJV). Paul knew what God called him to do and did it, without being deterred.

What would deter you and me? What would deflect us from the pursuit of our faith? What might turn us aside as followers of Jesus? Can smaller things, less difficult than a shipwreck, beatings, threats, lack of food, or abuse cause us to weaken our fervor? Probably so.

Paul's passion was to know Christ and to save others (Phil. 3:10; 1 Cor. 9:22). When the end of his life was near, he wrote, "I have fought the good fight, I have finished the race, I have kept the faith. Now there is [reserved] for me the crown of righteousness" (2 Tim. 4:7–8). He said, "I've done what God told me to do. I've finished the course. I'm going to be rewarded by God Himself." He saw past the distractions to the end result.

When he was visiting with his Ephesian leaders for the last time, Paul described his future: "I go bound in the spirit unto Jerusalem" (Acts 20:22 KJV). He felt constrained to go the way the Lord led him. Even his close colleagues tried to dissuade him. On his way there, he stopped at Tyre, where some of his disciples urged him not to go (Acts 21:4). They claimed that they had the Spirit of God when they cautioned him. But Paul would not be persuaded otherwise.

Once in Caesarea, Paul met a prophet by the name of Agabus. Agabus delivered a conflicting personal message to him. He took off Paul's belt and tied his own hands and feet with it. Then he said, "The Holy Spirit says, 'In this way the Jews of Jerusalem will bind the owner of this belt and will hand him over to the Gentiles'" (Acts 21:11). Everyone pleaded with Paul not to go. Paul's response? "Why are you weeping and breaking my heart? I am ready not only to be bound, but also to die in Jerusalem for the name of the Lord Jesus" (v. 13). So Paul fulfilled his orders. In Jerusalem, there was tumult and a great street scene. Paul was seized, a mob attempted to kill him, and the authorities put him in chains.

Agabus was right about what would happen. But he was not right about trying to persuade Paul not to go. Paul knew his course. He allowed nothing to get him off track. "I'm going to finish the course. Nothing will trip me up in any way. I'm going to look unto Jesus."

Not only was Paul determined in his service but also joyfully confident. He was encouraging the leadership of the church as he would never see them again, "Neither count I my life dear unto myself, so that I might finish my course with joy" (Acts 20:24 KJV). Wouldn't it be nice to finish the work of the Lord with such delight? When we realize and embrace the Lord's will for us, we will love to do it. We won't want to do anything else. It's a passion. Paul felt this, and he clung to it. He aimed to continue in the joy of the Lord from beginning to end.

Paul said, "I thank Christ Jesus our Lord, who hath enabled me, for that he counted me faithful, putting me into the ministry" (1 Tim. 1:12 KJV). Once we take on something, we're responsible for it. "It is required that those who have been given a trust must prove faithful" (1 Cor. 4:2). We serve the Lord, and we are to be consistent about it. Distractions—however severe they may be—should not keep us from our appointed task. Paul knew the secret to maintaining his mission: "One thing I do: Forgetting what is behind and straining toward what is ahead, I press on toward the goal to win the prize for which God has called me heavenward in Christ Jesus" (Phil. 3:13–14).

May we always say with Paul, "I count not my life dear unto myself. I will do whatever it takes to finish the course

He has assigned me." And, as Jesus said referring to the total sweep of Scripture and prophecy, "In the volume of the book it is written of me, I delight to do thy will, Oh my God" (Ps. 40:7–8 KJV).

Father, may we follow and serve You without distraction. As Jesus did everything that pleased You and took joy, even in the shame and pain of the Cross, so may we live without hesitation and to Your honor and glory. You are worthy, Lord. You only are our Strength and our Redeemer. In the name of the Lord Jesus, Amen.

13

Every Single Minute

From Miletus, Paul sent to Ephesus for the elders of the church. When they arrived, he said to them: "You know how I lived the whole time I was with you, from the first day I came into the province of Asia. I served the Lord with great humility and with tears, although I was severely tested by the plots of the Jews. You know that I have not hesitated to preach anything that would be helpful to you but have taught you publicly and from house to house. I have declared to both Jews and Greeks that they must turn to God in repentance and have faith in our Lord Jesus.

"And now, compelled by the Spirit, I am going to

Jerusalem, not knowing what will happen to me there. I only know that in every city the Holy Spirit warns me that prison and hardships are facing me. However, I consider my life worth nothing to me, if only I may finish the race and complete the task the Lord Jesus has given me—the task of testifying to the gospel of God's grace.

"Now I know that none of you among whom I have gone about preaching the kingdom will ever see me again. Therefore, I declare to you today that I am innocent of the blood of all men. For I have not hesitated to proclaim to you the whole will of God." (Acts 20:17—27)

The apostle Paul felt a great urgency to go to Jerusalem, although many counseled him not to make that trip. He wanted to finish the course and complete his ministry of testifying to the gospel of the grace of God. On the way, he stopped at Miletus and invited the elders from the church at Ephesus to visit him. Then he told them, "You know from the first day that I set my foot in Asia how I lived, serving the Lord. With all humility of mind, and with many tears and trials, I kept back nothing that was to your advantage. I taught you both publicly and privately."

Paul had an emotional tie to those men. He knew that he wouldn't return to them. This was a good-bye. Also, he was worried about the Ephesian church leaders—worried that they might fall short in their care and protection of the flock. So he wanted to urge them about their responsibilities to feed and lead, to warn and watch over the people. He reminded them of his leadership example: "Remember that for three years I never stopped warning each of you night and day with tears" (Acts 20:31). It wasn't an exaggeration. Paul did as he said. He possessed the rare quality of integrity.

There's nothing like the power of integrity. It is a characteristic so radiant, so steady, so consistent, so beautiful, that it makes a permanent picture in our minds. Paul wanted to look the Ephesian elders in the eye and affirm, "You had an example: I served the Lord."

Paul's service becomes more impressive—and more convicting—when we understand the implications of the word *servant*. The slave was one who was owned; he was the property of the master. Then if he was freed, he was called a "freeman." If the slave continued serving his former master, he did so voluntarily. "I can do whatever I want," he might say, "but my choice is to work for my master." That's the meaning of the word *servant:* service by choice. And all through the epistles, Paul identified himself as "the servant of Jesus Christ."

Serving requires skill and modesty. A servant is seen, but he shouldn't be obvious. He's in the background, he's available, he's always ready, he knows what to do. The servant anticipates what the master wants, like a good waiter does in a fine dining establishment. This is the way Paul served the Lord.

How prone we are to fail in this attitude toward our service for the Lord, even in ministry positions. Some people who haven't been called are in the business of Christianity. They are attracted by the promise of profit or popularity, or by an attractive career choice. A market-driven culture tends to drive spiritual movements, resulting in the loss of a heavenly vision of the call of God. We should feel cautioned and warned that in any ministry, as popular and successful as it may be, we must be sure our ultimate motivation is serving the Lord. Self-service brings God's judgment (1 Sam. 2:25–26).

Service should be wholehearted. Paul said, "In the ministry that the Lord has given to me, I have not held back." It sounds almost arrogant, but it wasn't. "I count not my life dear unto myself," he stated bluntly. Later, while in prison, he reiterated this commitment to the Philippians: "For to me, to live is Christ and to die is gain" (1:21). He knew the focal point of ministry was selfless service, even to the point of death for Jesus and the Gospel. "We are not trying to please men but God, who tests our hearts" (1Thess. 2:4).

We have a choice. Are we going to serve ourselves, or are we going to serve the Lord? First Corinthians 6:20 says, "You were bought at a price. Therefore honor God with your body." In Colossians 4:1, Paul put it even more pointedly: "You know that you . . . have a Master in heaven." Because we're bought with a price, we're free. Because we're free, we can choose to serve the Lord or not. Paul commanded that we serve as he did—steadfastly, without hesitation, despite tears and trials.

Someday we will be in the position Paul was in that day at Miletus. We will be on the verge of saying good-bye to this life and to those we have instructed in the faith. Wouldn't it be good if our parting words could be the same as his: "Every single minute I was with you, I served the Lord." May it be so.

Dear Father in Heaven, we remember Your Son who said, "I have not come to be served, but to serve and to give my life a ransom for many, and that the one that is great is the servant of all." May we serve You lovingly and faithfully, as Jesus did. In His holy name, Amen.

14

THE HALLMARK OF GOD'S SERVANT

As God's chosen people, holy and dearly loved, clothe yourselves with compassion, kindness, humility, gentleness and patience. (Colossians 3:12)

Show true humility toward all men. (Titus 3:2)

In humility consider others better than yourselves. (Philippians 2:3)

The preoccupation with self is the enemy of humility. We cannot lead people farther spiritually than we've come ourselves. If we are carnal people, we'll have carnal interests. If we are spiritual, we'll attract those who are seeking spiritual meaning. Our life pursuits will reflect our character and personal integrity. When money is lost, nothing is lost. When health is lost, something is lost. But when character is lost, all is lost.

Character and humility were qualities Paul both preached and lived. In Miletus, he said that he had "served the Lord with great humility and with tears" (Acts 20:19). When we read of his bold defense of the faith, his aggressive expansion of the Gospel, his assertive leadership style, and his contention for the whole Gospel, we wonder how he describes it as tearful and tender.

We are so often confused by the overemphasis on the self and our tendency toward self-affirmation that we may wonder how it is possible to be truly humble. Apparently, it is. Let's remember that we think truth before we experience it—it's in the mind. Humility starts in the thoughts. Paul wrote, "Let this mind be in you, which was also in Christ Jesus" (Phil. 2:5 KJV). Like a filter on a computer, a mindset of humility must block our pride. When we begin to think about what might cause us to "think of yourself more highly than you ought" (Rom. 12:3), we invite egotism, which is the affirmation of the self above God.

What is humility? The Bible states, "Now Moses was a very humble man, more humble than anyone else on the face of the earth" (Num. 12:3). It's hard to believe that he was humble or "meek." We picture Moses in great stature with a powerful personality and unequaled leadership, but we also remember his reluctance to lead and exert himself after God called him to return to Egypt (Ex. 3:11).

If Moses is a good example of humility, the people he was called to lead were not. It was their refusal to trust him and God to enter the land of promise that resulted in their wandering in the desert for forty years (Num. 14:21–23). Picture in your mind at least two million people constantly breaking camp day after day. The estimate is that it would have taken four hours just to get ready to walk, at least four hours of travel, and then two or three hours to settle down again at the end of the day with herds of animals and massive supplies. Every day of these forty years there were hundreds of funerals, and only those younger than twenty would enter the land except Joshua and Caleb. God was grinding down their pride.

In Deuteronomy 8:2, Moses reminds the Israelites: "[God] humbled you, causing you to hunger and then feeding you with manna." God used those forty years to humble them, to teach them to keep His commandments and to trust Him. Learning humility is a painful process. If we exalt ourselves, we will be put down, but if we humble ourselves, we will be exalted (Luke 14:11).

Humility is an attitude. It is an inner system of caution we should use to evaluate ourselves before the Lord. The Lord is high and lifted up, and we are supposed to take a position of lowliness. We think of the apostle Paul as assertive, bold, and confrontational. He was not passive. When Peter was compromising, Paul "opposed him to his face" (Gal. 2:11). This evangelist, strategist, and architect of church history seems anything but humble. Yet that was the quality he claimed for himself and preached to us (Phil. 4:7–8).

Paul reminded the Corinthians of his painful service: "All right, you Corinthians, I want to tell you my personal experience. I was whipped five times. I was beaten with rods three times. I was let down by a wall in a basket. I was stoned. I've been imprisoned. I've been naked. I've been lonely. I've been shipwrecked three times. I've been hungry. I've been deprived. I've been betrayed by other people" (see 2 Cor. 11:23–33). Yet, at the end of his ministry this man could say, "I'm the least of all the saints" (see Eph. 3:8).

The apostle James warned his readers against favoritism, a subtle form of pride. "If you show special attention to the man wearing fine clothes and say, 'Here's a good seat for you,' but say to the poor man, 'You stand there' or 'Sit on the floor by my feet,' have you not discriminated among yourselves and become judges with evil thoughts?" (2:3–4). I'll tell you what: those who are lowly God will exalt, and those who are rich God will put down. They will be like the flower of the field, and they will wither and die and blow away—they'll perish (see James 1:9–11).

Consider also how Ahab the king of Old Testament history "sold himself to do evil in the eyes of the LORD, urged on by Jezebel his wife. He behaved in the vilest manner" (1 Kings 21:25–26). God sent Elijah to confront Ahab and forecast destruction. Yet the king's response moved even God, whom he had insulted. "Have you noticed," he asked Elijah, "how Ahab has humbled himself before me? Because he has humbled himself, I will not bring this disaster in his day" (v. 29). How wonderfully encouraging that Ahab's humble response to chastening held back the judgment of God.

This is one of God's absolutely reliable principles for life: "If my people, which are called by my name, shall humble themselves, and pray, and seek my face, and turn from their wicked ways; then I will hear from heaven, and will forgive their sin" (2 Chron. 7:14 KJV). That's the power of humility, the power of taking the proper position before the Lord, and serving the Lord with humility of mind.

Consider the fall of Lucifer, the highest of angels. He saw the glory and the splendor of the Almighty and the angels that worshiped Him. But he wanted that for himself. Lucifer was the brightest angelic creation in the universe, but what did he do? He said, "I will be like the most high God. I will raise my throne. I will ascend above all." But God said to Satan, "You will be brought down" (see Isa. 14:12–15).

Pride entered the holiest of all places, heaven itself. Isn't that frightening? At the peak of our spiritual growth, in the tender moments of deep desire for God, selfish pride asks, "What's in it for me?" The Scripture says, "God opposes the proud, but gives grace unto the humble" (James 4:6).

God gives grace to the humble, not to the prideful. If we assume self-advancing attitudes, we've missed His gift of favor. "Humble yourselves therefore under the mighty hand of God, that he may exalt you in due time" (1 Peter 5:6 KJV). Personal humility is a spiritual discipline and the hallmark of the service of Jesus.

Father, thank You for Your Word. Help us to live it and to follow the example of the Lord Jesus, who humbled Himself and yielded willingly to the death of the Cross. Then You, oh God, exalted Him and gave Him a name that was above every other name. With broken and contrite hearts, we bow before You and pray that we may worship and serve You in the humility of our minds and hearts. In Jesus' name, Amen.

15

BE READY, FOR JESUS IS COMING AGAIN

[Jesus] was taken up before their very eyes, and a cloud hid him from their sight.

They were looking intently up into the sky as he was going, when suddenly two men dressed in white stood beside them. "Men of Galilee," they said, "why do you stand here looking into the sky? This same Jesus, who has been taken from you into heaven, will come back in the same way you have seen him go into heaven." (Acts 1:9–11)

The disciples stood at the scene of Jesus' ascension, absorbing His final words and contemplating what He meant. They were concentrating so intently on Jesus' disappearance that they were unaware of two men standing near them. The men, angels in human form, asked, "Why stand ye gazing up into heaven? This same Jesus, which is taken up from you into heaven, shall so come in like manner as ye have seen him go into heaven" (Acts 1:11 KJV).

Throughout Scripture, we read that He will in fact come back to the earth, as He said—"I am going away and I am coming back to you" (John 14:28). "For the Son of Man is going to come in his Father's glory with his angels" (Matt. 16:27). Many refer to it as "the imminent return of Christ," reflecting the possibility of His return at any moment.

The Word gives us very specific guidelines to follow as we wait for this event. To Timothy, Paul wrote, "In view of his appearing and his kingdom, I give you this charge: Preach the Word; be prepared in season and out of season; correct, rebuke and encourage—with great patience and careful instruction . . . Keep your head in all situations, endure hardship, do the work of an evangelist, discharge all the duties of your ministry" (2 Tim. 4:1–2, 5). He wrote also, "I charge you to keep this command without spot or blame until the appearing of our Lord Jesus Christ, which God will bring about in his own time" (1 Tim. 6:13–15).

In other words, *Think clearly. Be consistent and unswerving, even though it's difficult, and never fail to present the Gospel.* The result and consequences were inevitable for Paul and will be for every follower of Jesus Christ. "I have fought the good fight," he said, "I have finished the race, I have kept the faith. Now there is in store for me the crown of righteousness, which the Lord, the righteous Judge, will award to me on that day." The Lord will give such a crown to "all who have longed for his appearing" (2 Tim. 4:7–8).

Does the return of Jesus for His own excite you? The world we live in, with its many distractions, makes such a desire almost impossible, but we can't let our environment diminish the reality of the return of the Lord Jesus. Start to anticipate His appearing. Look forward to the day we will worship the King and all of the earth will submit to Him (Phil. 2:10–11). Jesus is coming not only to take us out of the world, but also to initiate His coronation, the moment when every knee will bow and every tongue will confess that He is Lord.

How, then, is a life lived in anticipation? How do we wait?

Be alert for His coming. Luke 12:37 says, "Blessed are those servants, whom the lord when he cometh shall find watching" (KJV). In a moment, in the twinkling of an eye, He'll come. Though many may say, "Our Lord delays His return. We've got time. All the leading indicators are not in place." This is the exact opposite of the expectant attitude commanded by Jesus for all of His followers.

Be holy. Paul prayed for the Thessalonians: "May He strengthen your hearts so that you will be blameless and holy in the presence of our God and Father when our Lord Jesus comes with all his holy ones" (1 Thess. 3:13). May our souls and bodies be ready for Him. It would be terrible to be doing something we would be ashamed of or be somewhere we should not be when He comes.

Be zealous. Titus 2 tells us to live godly lives in this present age, looking for and anticipating the appearance of Christ. For He redeemed us from all iniquities, that we might be purified as a people for Himself, zealous of good works. Be strong and boldly passionate, living for Christ and His kingdom.

Be confident. Scripture reminds us that we are in a battle—invisible, one not of flesh and blood but of principalities and powers and of spiritual wickedness in dark places (Eph. 6:12). However, the day of victory is coming. Satan and his angels will be deposited in the lake of fire, which burns with fire and brimstone forever and forever (Rev. 20:10). But we will be evacuated before global upheaval and the end of this age. Such a hope should give us vigor in battle.

Be an encouragement. "The dead in Christ will rise first. After that, we who are still alive and are left will be caught up . . . in the clouds to meet the Lord in the air. And so we will be with the Lord forever" (1 Thess. 4:16–17). We are to comfort one another with these words (v. 18).

Tell others. Jesus' last words to His disciples before He ascended were to commission them, "Ye shall be witnesses unto me both in Jerusalem, and in all Judaea, and in Samaria, and unto the uttermost part of the earth" (Acts 1:8 KJV). We must tell the world He is coming. The consequence of the

Gospel is the hope of heaven, and if it is then rejected, the results are eternal separation from God, and all that is good, forever.

"Why are you standing here gazing?" the men in radiance asked. They might have added, "Get going!"

"As you've seen Him taken up in the clouds, in like manner He will come back," those messengers said. Until then let's do the work of the faithful disciple. Let us be pure and watchful; let us tell others He is coming. Be bold and anticipate His appearing. And someday in glory, Christ Himself will hand a crown to all those who love His appearing (2 Tim 4:8).

The Lord is coming. *Maranatha!*

Father, we thank You and praise You that You are coming. You've not delayed; You have not put off Your promise. Your Word is settled in heaven, even every little dot and stroke of the pen. You will come again. In the meanwhile, make us more passionate and zealous, consistent and humble, as we proclaim that You are "the way, the truth and the life." We bow before You and wait Your return. All glory to the coming Lord Jesus. In His name, Amen.

16

UNCHANGING PRINCIPLES FOR LIFE

"Now I want you to know, brothers, that what has happened to me has really served to advance the gospel. As a result, it has become clear throughout the whole palace guard and to everyone else that I am in chains for Christ. Because of my chains, most of the brothers in the Lord have been encouraged to speak the word of God more courageously and fearlessly.

It is true that some preach Christ out of envy and rivalry, but others out of good will. The latter do so in love, knowing that I am put here for the defense of the gospel. The former preach Christ out of selfish ambition, not sincerely, supposing that they can stir up trouble for me while I am in chains. But what does it matter? The important thing is that in every way, whether from false motives or true, Christ is preached. And because of this I rejoice.

Yes, and I will continue to rejoice, for I know that through your prayers and the help given by the Spirit of Jesus Christ, what has happened to me will turn out for my deliverance. I eagerly expect and hope that I will in no way be ashamed, but will have sufficient courage so that now as always Christ will be exalted in my body, whether by life or by death." (Philippians 1:12—20)

The essence of the Christian life is Jesus: that in all things He might have the preeminence, not that in some things He might have a place. Our personal devotion must be more than just supplemental. Too many times in our study of the Scripture we're looking just for something to help us with our problems or to explain the many personal conflicts we face. It is typically human to turn to the Bible for selfish reasons. Instead of seeking simply to know

God and His purposes, we approach our Bibles for life application at the expense of adoration and praise.

The book of Philippians expresses this purpose in life. "For to me, to live is Christ and to die is gain" (1:21); "I consider everything a loss compared to the surpassing greatness of knowing Christ Jesus my Lord" (3:8); "I can do everything through him who gives me strength" (4:13). In every situation, Paul had learned contentment and resigned himself to accept every circumstance of life "for the excellency of the knowledge of Christ Jesus my Lord" (Phil. 3:8 KJV). All that mattered to him was the Gospel. If I die, I'll be with the Lord. If I'm here, so be it. But the purpose of my life is that "Christ shall be magnified in my body" (Phil. 1:20 KJV).

Where did Paul get the power to fulfill his purpose? He reflected that his power was not in physical strength, in achievements, in background, in academic wisdom, or genetic code. He considered all that he knew and accomplished as trash compared to his passion to know Jesus, the fellowship of His sufferings, and "the power of his resurrection" (3:4). Even the good can be an obstacle to the best.

That's where the power is. What propels, what sustains, is the living Christ Jesus. "I no longer live, but Christ lives in me" (Gal. 2:20). So the Christian life is not *simply* following principles but being empowered to fulfill our purpose: knowing and exalting Christ. However, biblical principles do give us a strategy, a blueprint, for achieving that goal. Two specific principles will enable us to be balanced, and they never need to change.

The first principle is to go beyond *immediates* to *ultimates*. Every time we are tempted in life it will be by an immediate. It will be something that will suggest to us that we need to postpone the more important for the more urgent or immediate. It will cause us to miss the goal. Immediates are the things that so easily sidetrack us and cause us to lose momentum for spiritual maturity.

What is the ultimate? Our relationship with God. Paul desired for every choice he made and action he took to advance this. He was pressing toward the prize, he said (Phil. 3:14), keeping his earthly distractions under control so that Christ might be all in all (1 Cor. 9:24–27).

Do we have this focus? This overriding, propelling purpose will exclude anything that hinders the supremacy of Jesus, His Gospel, or its global advancement. What are the ultimates in your life? And what are the extraneous things that should be eliminated?

The second principle is that, as followers of the Lord Jesus, we need to proceed beyond the knowledge of our *salvation* to our experience of our *sanctification*. What is sanctification? It comes from the word that means "to set apart." As we live set apart, we offset the corruptive influence of the world's systems, and we grow in holiness. To be holy means to be "totally given over to the Lord." This is not perfectionism, but honest introspection that asks, "Is there anything that holds me back from living a holy life that is Christlike?"

Sanctification is the all-encircling purpose of God, who "from the beginning chose you to salvation through sanctification of the Spirit and belief of the truth" (2 Thess. 2:13 KJV). It is the result of redemption (Titus 2:14) and is the energizing power for living. How is this power released? It begins with lifelong turning from sin and experiencing God's prevailing grace:

By the Word of God (John 17:17)

By the peace of God (1 Thess. 5:23)

By sexual purity (1 Thess. 4:3–4)

By total submission to the will of God (Rom. 12:1–2)

By maintaining a clear conscience (1 Peter 3:15–16)

By pursuing holiness (Heb. 12:14)

Take inventory of your life by personal self-examination that identifies your spiritual weaknesses. Ask the Lord for His grace to "be filled with the Spirit" (Eph. 5:18) and experience the joy of a pure heart (Matt 5:8).

Lord God, strengthen us in the pursuit of a life devoted to You. May Your Word enlighten us and Your Son be exalted, so that we will be "blameless and holy in the presence of our God and Father when our Lord Jesus comes with all His holy ones" (1 Thess. 3:13). In Jesus' name, Amen.

PART IV

ASSURANCE:

THE CERTAINTIES

OF OUR FAITH

17

SURE OF GOD, SURE OF SALVATION

Praise be to the God and Father of our Lord Jesus Christ! In his great mercy he has given us new birth into a living hope through the resurrection of Jesus Christ from the dead, and into an inheritance that can never perish, spoil or fade—kept in heaven for you, who through faith are shielded by God's power until the coming of the salvation that is ready to be revealed in the last time. In this you greatly rejoice, though now for a little while you may have had to suffer some grief in all kinds of trials. These have come so that your faith—of greater worth than gold, which perishes even though refined by fire—may be proved genuine and may result in praise, glory and honor when

Jesus Christ is revealed. Though you have not seen him, you love him; and even though you do not see him now, you believe in him and are filled with an inexpressible and glorious joy, for you are receiving the goal of your faith, the salvation of your souls. (1 Peter 1:3–9)

To have confidence in salvation is to understand what it means to be secure in the Lord. How can we be absolutely certain that on this hour and this day our sins are forgiven? How can we say that because our sins are forgiven, we're going to heaven and we know it? What does the Bible tell us about the guarantee of salvation?

First, we can be certain of our salvation because of the nature and the character of God. Any examination of the Scripture from Genesis to Revelation shows a pattern of human behavior: rebellion, ruin, repentance, and restoration. The Bible opens with a beautiful description of all that God had planned. It wasn't an afterthought; it was what He wanted to do in breathing upon the face of the waters and separating the mountains from the sea and forming all things in His creative power. What an amazing thought!

Then God said, "Let us make man in our image, in our likeness" (Gen. 1:26). But in man and woman sprang a root of resentment and resistance to God's instructions. The man and the woman disobeyed and sinned against God. They were driven by the angel with the sword from the garden, but with that judgment came the future promise that from the seed of the woman, in a future generation, would come a redeemer.

God gave the law and sent the prophets to convict people of sin and to hold mankind accountable. God said, "You've killed all My servants and ignored My prophets. I'll send My Son." With Jesus, came the fulfillment of the law and the ultimate deliverance: "The law was given by Moses, but grace and truth came by Jesus Christ" (John 1:17 KJV) so that "as many as received him, to them gave he power to become the sons of God, even to them that believe on his name" (John 1:12 KJV). "For God so loved the world that he gave his one and only Son, that whoever believes in him shall not perish but have eternal life" (John 3:16).

The nature of God is that He's a saving God, "not willing that any should perish" (2 Peter 3:9 KJV). "Come, all you who are weighted down by life. Come because your burdens are so heavy. Everyone who is weary," Jesus said, "just come and I'll give you rest" (see Matt. 11:28).

Here is the nature and character of a giving and loving God, who says that He will give His Son in order to give you rest, to give you freedom from the bondage of sin, and to give you freedom from His judgment and from hell. But if you want to settle for less, for the fleeting pleasures of this world or for being in control of your life, the consequences and the results are in your hands. His desire is to give to all who receive His Son mercy and grace. Will you believe and accept by faith this awesome salvation?

Second, we can be certain of salvation because of the extent and condition of this salvation. The extent is to all people, and the requirement is faith. Paul wrote to Timothy of "God our Savior, who wants all men to be saved" (1 Tim. 2:3–4). Ephesians 2:8–9 says, "For it is by grace you have been saved, through faith—and this not from yourselves, it is the gift of God—not by works, so that no one can boast."

Human efforts that seek to impress God or persuade Him to overlook sin are insults to a God of grace.

Grace is a gift that we don't deserve. We can't earn our salvation. We have to have faith that Jesus is the sole Savior, that He is the way. Jesus didn't say, "I'll show you the way" or "I'm one of the many ways." He says, "I am the way and the truth" (John 14:6). God's salvation comes as a gift; it is eternal, and it is a continuum, meaning it starts when I receive the gift in faith and is never-ending.

Salvation isn't start-and-stop with God. When we receive the gift, we are saved. Salvation isn't a past-tense experience; salvation is present and forever. "Through faith [we] are shielded by God's power until the coming of the salvation that is ready to be revealed" (1 Peter 1:5). His mercy, His justice, His equity—all that God has for us will never cease because we have become one with Christ. Jesus said, "I am the resurrection, and the life . . . whosoever liveth and believeth in me shall never die" (John 11:25–26 KJV).

Salvation is now and forever—free by God's grace, flowing from the nature and the character of God. This is never-ending security.

Father, we thank You that You are our God forever and ever, and that You have allowed us to step into the continuum of Your saving power. We thank You that salvation will never be withdrawn. You are immutable; You cannot change; and You cannot break Your promise of eternal salvation. We thank You that whoever will call on Your name will be saved. In Jesus' precious name, Amen.

18

The Shepherd and His Sheep

"I tell you the truth, the man who does not enter the sheep pen by the gate, but climbs in by some other way, is a thief and a robber. The man who enters by the gate is the shepherd of his sheep. The watchman opens the gate for him, and the sheep listen to his voice. He calls his own sheep by name and leads them out. When he has brought out all his own, he goes on ahead of them, and his sheep follow him because they know his voice. But they will never follow a stranger; in fact, they will run away from him because they do not recognize a stranger's voice." Jesus used this figure of speech, but they did not understand what he was telling them.

Therefore Jesus said again, "I tell you the truth. I am the gate for the sheep. All who ever came before me were thieves and robbers, but the sheep did not listen to them. I am the gate; whoever enters through me will be saved. He will come in and go out, and find pasture. The thief comes only to steal and kill and destroy; I have come that they may have life, and have it to the full.

"I am the good shepherd. The good shepherd lays down his life for the sheep. The hired hand is not the shepherd who owns the sheep. So when he sees the wolf coming, he abandons the sheep and runs away. Then the wolf attacks the flock and scatters it. The man runs away because he is a hired hand and cares nothing for the sheep.

"I am the good shepherd; I know my sheep and my sheep know me—just as the Father knows me and I know the Father—and I lay down my life for the sheep . . .

"I give them eternal life, and they shall never perish; no one can snatch them out of my hand. My Father, who has given them to me, is greater than all; no one can snatch them out of my Father's hand." (John 10:1–15, 28–29)

How can we identify the Shepherd's sheep? How do we recognize the sheep from the wolves? If someone says he is a true believer, what are the marks of authenticity that verify his claim? John 10 shows us how we can tell who is part of Jesus' flock.

There are ten descriptions in this passage of true believers in the Good Shepherd. First, it tells us the sheep are enclosed; it speaks about the sheepfold in verse 1. Second, we read that the sheep "hear." Third, the sheep have names; the Shepherd "knows them." Fourth, the sheep are "led." Fifth, the sheep are guided "by the Good Shepherd."

Sixth, the Shepherd goes before His sheep. Anything we ever undertake for the Lord we should do remembering John 10:4: "And when he puts forth his own sheep, he goes before them, and the sheep follow him." The Lord is in our tomorrows. He is the antecedent of everything.

Seventh, the sheep know the Shepherd's voice. Eighth, the sheep go in and out and find pasture. Ninth, the sheep have life because He gives it to them. And tenth, the Shepherd gives His life for the sheep (v. 11). These are the characteristics of the sheep of the Good Shepherd. The spiritual implications of this teaching of Jesus about the sheep are noted by Peter, who was given the charge to shepherd the flock of God, that the true sheep "are kept by the power of God through faith unto salvation" (I Pet. 1:5 KJV) and will never perish (John 10:28).

Ask a person claiming to be Christian, "What do you believe in?" The object of faith is more important than just believing. You can believe in anything. Faith has an object. It is placed in something or someone. Our faith is in God's Son and His wonderful work. Our hope as sheep is in Jesus, the Shepherd—nothing more, nothing less, nothing else.

The Shepherd is sovereign; He doesn't change His mind or lie. He does not alter or renege, changing the conditions of His word. No. All of our salvation rests on the immutability of God—the impossibility for God to change. The changelessness of God is the foundation of the believer's stability. A person calling himself one of Christ's sheep will show confidence in God's perfection.

Saving faith is not a blind trust; it has to be reasonable and consistent. All faith in Christ meets the criteria of the mind. That's why when we hear the Word, we don't necessarily "feel" it. We think it through, and faith is born. Faith comes by hearing the Word of God (Rom. 10:17). Christianity is rational. Jesus Christ the Shepherd makes sense to the sheep.

Faith means we believe in the Savior. "Whosoever shall call on the name of the Lord shall be saved" (Acts 2:21 KJV). God calls us through our consciences. He calls through nature's patterns and cycles. He calls through preaching. He calls through circumstances. He calls through sorrow. He calls through our reasoning. And if you answer Him, if you believe in Him and call on Him to be your Shepherd Savior, you pass from judgment and condemnation to eternal life (John 5:24). The sheep are those who hear the call, believe, and are saved.

Sheep respond to the call of salvation, and they continue to respond to the Shepherd's voice. They hear; they receive; they listen; they follow; they're fed, they're enfolded. The loving Shepherd precedes them as they go in and out and find nourishment. There's a stability about these sheep-persons; they remain at the side of the Shepherd. This is why salvation is secure. A sheep-person has fellowship. We recognize God's sheep as those who maintain this ongoing relationship with Jesus, the Shepherd. "My sheep hear my voice, and I know them, and they follow me" (John 10:27 KJV).

The sheep are not only the believing followers of Jesus but also those who place complete faith in the Shepherd's sacrifice. "I give unto them eternal life; and they shall never perish" (John 10:28 KJV). They're in my hand. My hand is in the Father's hand, and nobody is able to pluck them out (see v. 29). No adversary, no angel, nor Satan or any demon, no circumstance or sin can remove us from the safety of our Shepherd's fold. Jesus' sheep know they never will lose their salvation. Nobody can take away what God gives.

Our responsibility is to feed from Him, to stay close to Him, to follow Him—because sheep easily go astray—so that we eternally experience the protection and companionship of our Great Shepherd the Lord Jesus Christ.

> *Father, we're humbled to realize how wonderful was the gift of Your Son. You not only save us from the judgment, but also know the needs of our hearts. We are prone to wander and continue to feel the lure of the enemy of our souls and to leave the*

love of the Shepherd. We thank You that Your great care for us keeps us safe in the strong hands of Your Son, who has placed His hands in Yours with the promise that we can never be lost and that we have life forever. In the incomparable name of Jesus, Amen.

19

WE ARE CALLED

To those who have been called, who are loved by God the Father and kept by Jesus Christ: Mercy, peace, and love be yours in abundance. (Jude 1–2)

Another certainty of the Christian life is that God wants us to be saved; therefore, He is constantly calling. Jude began his little epistle with a greeting "to those who have been called."

There are several "calls" in Scripture. The first is the general call that comes from nature. We see this in Psalm

19:1: "The heavens declare the glory of God; and the firmament shews his handywork" (KJV). That sound and voice are everywhere in the world, and everyone hears it. The world, space, and all visible components reverberate with God's presence and demonstrate His mighty power.

We find the same appeal described in Romans 1:20: "For the invisible things of him from the creation of the world are clearly seen, being understood by the things that are made, even his eternal power and Godhead; so that they are without excuse" (KJV). Space, the stars, the moon, the sky, the ocean, and all aspects of our world reveal God in nature. Every human being knows this revelation instinctively, but, because of sin, represses it in their minds and hearts. That's why the psalmist explains this self-inflicted spiritual blindness: "The fool says in his heart, 'There is no God'" (Ps. 14:1). The human race is without excuse and guilty before God because of the sufficiency of the evidence (Rom. 3:19).

The second call is that of the Holy Spirit. It's the call of conviction. He convicts the world of sin, what is wrong, testifies to righteousness, what is right, and warns of judgment and the inevitable consequences (John 16:8). We are all guilty at some level, and repeated sin silences guilt. It creates a hardness of heart so that guilt doesn't result in regret or repentance. Departure from God becomes pleasurable wickedness and total disregard for the divine. Sin is especially self-destructive because it closes our heart to God's call.

The third is the call of Jesus or the call of the gospel. Every time the gospel is presented it is a summons. We find this call in the Old Testament as well. For instance, in Isaiah 1:18 God says, "Come now, let us reason together." Isaiah 55:1 invites, "Come, all you who are thirsty, come to the waters; and you who have no money, come, buy and eat!"

In the New Testament gospels, Jesus said, "Come" (Matt. 11:28). Throughout time God is intervening, moving in His divine acts, demonstrating His love, seeking the lost sheep of the house of Israel. Now Jesus comes as the Son of God in the new covenant saying, "[I] have come to seek and to save" (Luke 19:10). So we have the call of the natural world and the cosmos, the Law and the prophets, the perpetual call of the Holy Spirit, and the call of Christ: "Come to me, [everyone] . . . and I will give you rest" (Matt. 11:28).

The fourth call is conversion. Those who heed the call enjoy eternal salvation: "All that the Father gives me will come to me, and whoever comes to me I will never drive away" (John 6:37) and "Everyone who calls on the name of the Lord will be saved" (Rom. 10:13).

"He that believeth on the Son hath everlasting life: and he that believeth not the Son shall not see life; but the wrath of God abideth on him" (John 3:36 KJV). So the consequences of our response to the call are undeniable. Anyone can come, if he will; but all will not come. Faith in Jesus is what separates the called and chosen.

Call is an interesting word. One part of the word's meaning is "invited"; the other part of the word is "appointed." Here is this twin attribute of God. He invites, and those who respond on the condition of faith and belief He designates as His chosen ones (Matt. 22:14). It's profound, but both sides are there. That's why the gospel is so fair. Nobody will be able to say, "I wanted to be in heaven but ended up in hell." Everyone has the choice of whether or not to respond to the call.

If anyone doesn't believe, the consequences are the

result of his disbelief. That's not arbitrary. Paul writes to the first Christians in the great city of Thessalonica, "We ought always to thank God for you, brothers loved by the Lord, because from the beginning God chose you to be saved through the sanctifying work of the Spirit *and* through belief in the truth. He called you to this through our gospel, that you might share in the glory of our Lord Jesus Christ" (2 Thess. 2:13–14, emphasis added).

We can read it both ways: "From the beginning God chose us to be saved," and "He chose us to be saved through belief in the truth." He chose us to be saved by means of believing the truth, and by believing the truth the Holy Spirit sets us apart—that's the meaning of *sanctification*—"But you were washed, you were sanctified, you were justified in the name of the Lord Jesus Christ" (1 Cor. 6:11).

God says, "I call you." It is by the calling and the receiving of the gospel—the life, death, and resurrection of the Lord Jesus—that we receive eternal life. "Not by works of righteousness which we have done, but according to his mercy he saved us, by the washing of regeneration, and renewing of the Holy Ghost" (Titus 3:5 KJV).

We can all humbly say in the sincerity of faith, "I am loved; I am called; I am secure."

Father, we bless You, and because of Your Son, we give You praise and glory that we are kept by Your power and can rest in Your love. Your prevailing grace from eternity has never failed to continue to call everyone to receive Your salvation. We thank You for Your Holy Spirit, who has opened our hearts to receive and enables us to receive Your Son and to understand the mystery of the Gospel. In Jesus' name, Amen.

20

WE BELONG TO GOD

"Who shall separate us from the love of Christ?" (Romans 8:35)

"How great is the love the Father has lavished on us, that we should be called children of God!" (1 John 3:1)

"I will remain in the world no longer, but they are still in the world, and I am coming to you. Holy Father, protect them by the power of your name." (John 17:11)

The security of the Christian faith is God's love. When we say God's love, are we trying to express all that it encompasses? First, God's love anticipates our need of Him. "While we were still sinners, Christ died for us" (Rom. 5:8); Romans 5:10 says, "When we were God's enemies." God's affirmation came when we were the complete opposite of what He is. There couldn't be anything more inconceivable than a sinner relating to and being connected to a holy God. But His love offsets that: "While we were still sinners, Christ died for us."

Second, God's love is commitment: "I have loved you with an everlasting love" (Jer. 31:3). Love is not simply a feeling; love is also a commitment. If you want to express love to someone, you do something to show your love for that person. Jesus shocked people when he said to love your enemies, bless them, do good to them, and pray for them (see Luke 6:27–28). Such commands are astounding because those actions run counter to our sense of retaliation, but is that not exactly how God loves us?

Third, God's love is permanent. Our Lord is asking us,

"Do you want to know how much I love you? I love you like a woman who is nursing her child. Could a nursing mother ever give up her child? I will never do that" (see Isa. 49:15). God says, "I have engraved you on the palms of my hands" (Isa. 49:16). A tattoo is indelible, a visible mark. Every time you see a tattoo, think that God has tattooed you on His hands. It is the permanent marking that you are His. "Can I leave you?" God asks. "No. I can never do that. This is my love for you." The eternal God must be what He always is, unchanging in His fidelity. That is His character.

Fourth, God's love is inseparable. What or who can get between God and us? Pick a possibility. Angels? Principalities? Powers? The present? The future? Think of anything. What can cut us off from the love of our Father? "Nothing," said Paul. "We are more than conquerors through him who loved us" (Rom. 8:37). God's love is invincible.

The apostle John summed up this love by saying, "What manner of love the Father hath bestowed upon us" (1 John 3:1 KJV)! The language suggests that he was saying, "I'm out of words. What manner of love has the Father toward us? I can't describe it."

What would cause us to reject or abandon this great love? Why would anyone refuse to know the love of God and to live without Him, to be separated from His love and all that is good forever in Hell? It's unthinkable.

The fifth aspect of God's love is that He will *keep* us. We are so loved by God; we enjoy His supernatural protection. "[You] are kept by the power of God through faith unto salvation ready to be revealed in the last time" (1 Peter 1:5 KJV). Depositing our faith in Jesus Christ means God is now responsible for us, because He has purchased us. That's the meaning of the word *redeemed*. He bought us. We are His property. He paid dearly for us with the life of His Son, so He will never lose or reject us.

Paul testified to this value we hold when he wrote, "You are not your own; you were bought with a price" (1 Cor. 6:19–20). Our response? "Therefore, glorify God in your body, and in your spirit, which are God's" (v. 20 KJV). Christ bought your soul and your body; that's why the body is resurrected. He purchased us with the precious blood of His Son, who died and rose again. We will see the final redemption because anything God secures, He cannot lose.

This word "kept" is a military term that means "to seal, to guard, to keep under constant surveillance." The Lord watches over us. Here's the security of our faith. Here's the comfort of being saved. Here's our hope; it's in God who keeps us now and forever: "I give unto them eternal life; and they shall never perish, neither shall any man pluck them out of my hand" (John 10:28 KJV).

Not only did Jesus buy us with His blood, not only has He secured us in eternity, but He also urges the Father to keep us. Twice Jesus prayed, "Protect them by the power of your name . . . While I was with them, I protected them and kept them safe . . . My prayer is not that you take them out of the world but that you protect them from the evil one" (John 17:11–12, 15).

Evil will not defeat His own. We carry the seed of eternal life. We're partakers of the divine nature. Sin shouldn't even be of interest to us because Christ lives in us, and the Holy Spirit reigns in our lives. "No one who is born of God will continue to sin, because God's seed remains in him; he cannot go on sinning, because he has been born of God" (1 John 3:9). Worldly behavior should disgust us, nauseate us. It should offend us. It was said of Lot that wickedness vexed his soul. Is sin repulsive to you?

If we continue to practice what we know is offensive to God, we should evaluate our salvation. Because He is holy, we have to be holy. God protects us against the evil one, but we can choose to drift away, sinfully enticed to our own hurt. "Examine yourselves to see whether you are in the faith; test yourselves" (2 Cor. 13:5).

Of course God answers Jesus' prayer. Of course He can keep us from evil, if we live in His strength: "Be strong in the Lord, and in the power of his might. Put on the whole armour of God (Eph. 6:10–11 KJV). He's able to do "exceeding abundantly above all that we ask or think, according to the power that worketh in us" (Eph. 3:20 KJV). We are complete in Him. We are hid, covered with Christ in God, and we will be presented to God holy, without blame or fault in His sight (see Col. 2:10; 3:3; 1:22). God's love in Jesus Christ anticipates our needs. It is inseparable and eternal. We will never perish in the life to come, and we can know His mercy and His protection everyday until we see heaven. As the apostle marveled, what manner of love is this!

Father, Your love is almost impossible to conceive because it is so unconditional. You accept us, care for us, and keep us. You love us permanently. Thank You for our salvation. Our prayers seem so inadequate to express how wonderfully reassuring is this salvation. Above all, we marvel that it comes by Your grace when we believe and accept Your Son the Lord Jesus. We pray that we will live in godly gratitude for Your amazing love. In Jesus' name, Amen.

21

WE HAVE GOD'S PROMISE

When God made his promise to Abraham, since there was no one greater for him to swear by, he swore by himself, saying, "I will surely bless you and give you many descendants." And so after waiting patiently, Abraham received what was promised.

Men swear by someone greater than themselves, and the oath confirms what is said and puts an end to all argument. Because God wanted to make the unchanging nature of his purpose very clear to the heirs of what was promised, he confirmed it with an oath. God did this so that, by two unchangeable things in which it is impossible for God to lie, we who have fled to take hold of the hope offered to us may be greatly *encouraged. We have this hope as an anchor for the soul, firm and secure. (Hebrews 6:13–19)*

A promise is a verbal contract; it is an expression of surety or guarantee. A promise is not always applicable in the present but more expected to be in the future. Its power depends entirely on the character of the person making it. The promise has credibility only in the capacity of the person to guarantee it.

If a person's character is untrustworthy, if you are a person who hedges or lies, the promise is worthless. If you are a reliable person, your promise is trustworthy, but still not guaranteed. We are all human and make mistakes, and we don't always have the ability to follow through on promises that we make. But God's character is perfect, and He has the complete capacity to guarantee any promise that He makes.

God made a promise to Abraham: "I will make your offspring like the dust of the earth . . . No longer will you be called Abram; your name will be Abraham, for I have made you a father of many nations . . . all peoples on earth will be blessed through you" (Gen. 13:16; 17:5; 12:3).

The promise was an immutable covenant for a land, a nation, a kingdom, and a Redeemer. We read these prophecies in Genesis, the first book of the Bible, and they are being fulfilled in our lifetime. But it was God who gave the promise, so they were also certain to come to pass.

We saw the verification of God's guarantee in Abraham's life; Scripture records that "after he had patiently endured, he obtained the promise" (Heb. 6:15 KJV). Notice that there is a gap between when God gave the promise and when Abraham received it. This is true of many promises. When someone says he is going to do something, a waiting period is often anticipated.

That time spent in waiting for a promise to be fulfilled is when faith envisions the outcome. It's in that gap that we can delight God. Without this kind of faith, it's impossible to please God (Heb. 11:6). In this interval, we trust the one making the promise. Faith is trusting what is said and trusting the person who said it. Faith is defined as "the substance of things hoped for, the evidence of things not seen" (Heb. 11:1 KJV). Both definitions imply a current absence of the thing being hoped for and a confidence that it will eventually take place.

We are "heirs" of God's promise (Heb. 6:17). An heir is someone who is promised to receive something. We create heirs when we sign a document called a will, usually in the presence of witnesses, entitling certain possessions of ours to family and friends upon our death. The Lord Jesus provided a last will and testament. The witnesses are the Holy Spirit and God the Father. The Trinity agrees; no one can alter the conditions. The promise designating us as heirs has eternal value based on the quality and the capacity of God, who made the agreement. When Christ died, His will became effective. We have become His heirs.

Hebrews 6:17–18 tells us that "Because God wanted to make the unchanging nature of his purpose very clear . . . he confirmed it with an oath. God did this so that, by two unchangeable things, in which it is impossible for God to lie, we who have fled to take hold of the hope offered to us may be greatly encouraged." In other words, "I have made a promise," God says. His capacity, His capability, and His character are flawless. Therefore His promise is based on who He is. He cannot lie. He cannot abrogate. He cannot deceive. He cannot deny Himself. He cannot change. He cannot revise or go back on His Word.

He made an oath to confirm the promise. "I am God. I gave My oath, and it is immutable because I cannot lie."

He did this to "greatly encourage" us. "We have this hope as an anchor for the soul, firm and secure" (v. 19). There are fifteen different words for this word that we translate "hope." Hope is absolute assurance. The word has no doubt or hesitation in it. When we say, "My hope is in the Lord," look at the object of the hope. We can have full confidence in God's promises because we can have full faith in His character.

The hope in Romans 8:24 is a saving hope—it brings salvation. In 1 Peter 1:3, it's the living hope. It's reality. It's a relevant, applicable, perpetual, and eternal confidence in God. In Titus 1:2, it's a secure hope. In 1 Thessalonians 1:3, a patient hope. In Colossians 1:27, a glorious hope. In Romans 15:13, a hope that abounds. In Titus 2:13, it's a blessed hope. Romans 12:12 speaks of a joyful hope. We are told in 1 John 3:3 that the person who has this confidence keeps himself morally clean. It is a purifying hope.

The text calls our hope an "anchor." The hope we have in Jesus is the anchor for the soul—something sure and steadfast, preventing drifting or giving way, lowered to the depth of God's love. Christ is our Anchor. Through all of the crises of life—and we all are going to experience them— we have this magnificent Anchor. This hope has sustained all the patriarchs, martyrs, and all the followers of Jesus through all their conflicts from the Creation to now, and it will until eternity.

Heavenly Father, You are always so consistent and true to Your Word. Again, I give myself to You, body, soul, and spirit, and ask You to renew and revive my heart. Your word is my confidence, Your Son is my Anchor and for this I am forever grateful. In Jesus' precious and holy name, Amen.

PART V

PRAYER:

ACCESS TO THE

HEART OF GOD

22

LEARNING PRAYER FROM JESUS

"Lord, teach us to pray." (Luke 11:1)

When Jesus performed a miracle, the disciples didn't ask, "How can we do that?" They had been given similar power. They never requested His instruction on the best way to challenge the Pharisees. Only when He prayed did they say, "Lord, teach us." What was it about Jesus' prayers that made the disciples ask the question?

The New Testament records only five of Jesus' prayers. The first is what we call the Lord's Prayer (Matt. 6:9–13;

Luke 11:2–4). The second is the prayer in Matthew 11 in which He said, "I praise you, Father, Lord of heaven and earth, because you have hidden these things from the wise and learned, and revealed them to little children" (v. 25). The third is the most profound and awesome prayer in John 17, in which He prayed "for all those who will believe in me" in the future (v. 20). He prayed the fourth prayer alone at Gethsemane, where He submitted to the will of His Father (Luke 22:42). And then He spoke the fifth prayer from the cross: "Father, forgive them; for they know not what they do" (Luke 23:34 KJV).

Other than these examples, our Lord prayed alone, privately and away from people. Yet it was His praying that impressed the disciples and caused them to ask, "Lord, teach us to pray."

Think about their question. Did they mean, "Lord, teach us to pray like You just prayed?" Were they referring to His posture in prayer? We assume that when He prayed at the Last Supper, He was standing or sitting. Our Lord knelt when He prayed in the garden. And He prayed on the cross, where He was stretched out. Personal posture has nothing to do with the effectiveness of prayer although it can portray an attitude of the heart as kneeling shows humility and raised hands show surrender.

Was it His emotion, His passion, His brevity, or His simplicity? Was He praying tenderly? Was He praying softly? Was it the inflection of His voice? What was it about Jesus' prayer that made His disciples want to learn to pray like Him?

No matter what it was, the Lord answered them. He said, "*When* you pray . . ." The Lord assumed here that prayer would be part of our lives. He did not say, "If you pray." He expected prayer to be the natural, ongoing desire of life. Paul assumed this also, "Pray without ceasing" (1 Thess. 5:17). "In everything, . . . pray" (Phil. 4:6). Do you and I think that way? When we get up each morning, do we launch our day with prayer, or is prayer like dialing 911 only in emergencies, to get us through some crisis? Our Lord assumed we would be praying, and shouldn't we? Prayer ought to precede anything we do.

Jesus also told the disciples, "When you pray, go into your room" (Matt. 6:6). He was counteracting the

Pharisees' habit of praying in public for show so they would be noticed. The preface to prayer is humility. It is best when unnoticed by others.

Jesus also instructed them that words repeatedly said doesn't guarantee they are being heard (Matt. 6:7). Unrehearsed prayers tend to be more real and honest. Structure stifles spontaneity. We speak the Lord's name and come into His presence. "Your Father sees and hears your prayers and will reward you," Jesus said. When we pray, we do so in the authority of Jesus' name. We must remember that our only access in prayer is in the name of Jesus and not in the merit of the act of our praying.

A third insight we see in Jesus' example is that He frequently went to an isolated place to pray. He left even His ministry to the people to pray privately. "Very early in the morning, while it was still dark, Jesus got up, left the house and went off to a solitary place, where he prayed" (Mark 1:35). Do you have a place where you meet the Lord privately, where you can be alone with God? An old hymn reminds us, "There is a place of quiet rest, near to the heart of God . . . O Jesus, blest Redeemer, sent from the heart of God, hold us who wait before Thee near to the heart of God."[1]

Solitude and rest are related. You and I will find that when we are frustrated, stressed, irritable, forgetful, detached, or annoyed, the cause is that we're not rested. We need a time alone when we can restore our soul by praying. Prayer brings peaceful healing and renewal. It is the most intimate spiritual relationship with God. Jeremiah once asked, "Is there no balm in Gilead? Is there no physician there? Why then is there no healing for the wound of my people?" (8:22). For us the salve, the ointment that soothes the irritations of life, is Jesus Christ, the Great Physician. And we have instant communication with Him through times of prayerful solitude.

"Teach us to pray," the disciples said. And God's Word reassures, "Come boldly unto the throne of grace, that we may [receive] mercy, and find grace to help in time of need" (Heb. 4:16 KJV).

Father, teach us to pray. We're so immediate, so hurried, so cosmopolitan, so caught up in the now. We have to offset that,

Lord, with quietness and peace. Help us to do it in our lives. Please Lord, teach us to pray with calm attitudes, with restful spirits, and yet with urgency so we know that when we ask anything in Your name, You will do it. In Christ's name, Amen.

23

APPROPRIATE PRAYER

Then Jesus told his disciples a parable to show them that they should always pray and not give up. He said: "In a certain town there was a judge who neither feared God nor cared about men. And there was a widow in that town who kept coming to him with the plea, 'Grant me justice against my adversary.'

"For some time he refused. But finally he said to himself, 'Even though I don't fear God or care about men, yet because this widow keeps bothering me, I will see that she gets justice, so that she won't eventually wear me out with her coming!'"

And the Lord said, "Listen to what the unjust judge says. And will not God bring about justice for his chosen ones, who cry out to him day and night? Will he keep putting them off? I tell you, he will see that they get justice, and quickly. However, when the Son of Man comes, will he find faith on the earth?"

To some who were confident of their own righteousness and looked down on everybody else, Jesus told this parable: "Two men went up to the temple to pray, one a Pharisee and the other a tax collector. The Pharisee stood up and prayed about himself. 'God, I thank you that I am not like other men—robbers, evildoers, adulterers—or even like this tax collector. I fast twice a week and give a tenth of all I get.'

"But the tax collector stood at a distance. He would not even look up to heaven, but beat his breast and said, 'God, have mercy on me, a sinner.'

"I tell you that this man, rather than the other, went home justified before God. For everyone who exalts himself will be humbled, and he who humbles himself will be exalted." (Luke 18:1—14)

Prayer seems to be the most elusive discipline of the Christian life. We find it much easier to do other things. Prayer becomes a last resort, mostly unscheduled, and done when convenient rather than being a daily regimen. It seems intrusive and the least productive. Activity always seems more important: getting things done. But *being* is more important than *doing*. However, there is nothing you can do that brings you more in focus with yourself than prayer. It is one with God. Prayer is more than meditation; it becomes the unique opportunity for personal examination at the most intimate level. Prayer is not a weakness but a strength. Its benefits are patience, insight, endurance, and the power to cope with anything.

Jesus told a story about a very persistent widow, teaching that we should always pray and not give up. The woman had been abused *and* neglected—no one was taking up her case. Nobody was speaking up for her. Finally she decided, *I can't handle this anymore. I'm going to the judge.* She went to court, but the judge paid no attention to her. Yet, she still did not give up. She returned to the court again and again, pleading, "Look, I need somebody to speak up for me. I need a representative. Help me." And finally, even though the judge really didn't care about her case, her relentless pleas caused him to answer her and settle the complaint.

Because all parables have parallels, our first instinct might be to think that God is the judge and the woman is the believer, that we are an annoyance to such a mighty God. But we quickly learn that Jesus has a more wise purpose for crafting this parable as He did. *Unlike* the judge, God does care. He doesn't put anyone off. He hears, and He answers because it pleases him to do so, not just because He wants us to stop pestering Him. The Lord Jesus concludes the story by saying, "How much more do you think God responds to His elect, those He's chosen, who cry night and day unto Him?" (see Luke 18:7).

The key to the story is that this woman never quit. No, she never let up. She was annoying the judge by continuously coming to him for help, and she was shameless about it! She didn't care what the judge thought about her. She had a problem, and she was going to get it solved.

The teaching about prayer for us is that we should put aside doubts about prayers being answered, fears that we won't be heard, and thoughts that we are just a bother to God. It's just the opposite. He is always eager for us to come to Him to ask His help. We are the ones that, usually, are not interested in calling on Him. In the text, Jesus asked, "When the Son of Man comes, will He find faith on the earth?" Will we believe that God wants to hear and answer our prayers, or will we give up on Him and try to find our own solutions?

In this story, Jesus taught that when we pray, we should not let up, especially when there are few, if any, solutions. The tendency to give up indicates that asking doesn't make a difference and is probably not going to change anything. So, whatever we are praying for, Jesus is saying, is heard by God and circumstances do change but prayer should still be persistent. Don't ever be hesitant or embarrassed to pray. Just go to God with your need.

Jesus continues with the story of two men who went up to the temple to pray. One man was a Pharisee, a religious leader people resented, the other a tax collector, a person people hated. The Pharisee said, "I'm glad that I'm not an extortionist. I'm glad that I'm not unjust. I'm glad that I'm not an adulterer." In other words, "I'm righteous." But Jesus said, "He prayed about himself," and he stood farther away from the others, implying that he thought he was better than them. Religious pride and preference received the greatest rebukes from Jesus. The Pharisee was elevating and separating himself from those around him as well as looking down on them. The story was told to convict people who trust in their own righteousness.

Now look at the tax collector. He was standing too, but he couldn't look up. He was humbling himself. He was beating his chest, a common practice of heart-felt sorrow. He was saying, "God, I'm putting myself down. Please, don't You put me down." He used the word "mercy." He asked, "Don't give me what I deserve. God, be merciful to me a sinner," just seven words. Jesus said, "This man who exalted himself will be put down, but he who put himself down shall be exalted."

God says, "[My] name is holy: I live in a high and holy place, but also with him who is contrite and lowly in spirit" (Isa. 57:15). Humble prayers are the ones God hears.

If we humble ourselves and realize our bankruptcy before God, our need for His salvation and His help, if we come to prayer shamelessly and relentlessly, we will be expressing the appropriate attitudes for effective praying.

Father, help us to make prayer a desire, not a duty. We thank You, Lord, that You don't need complicated phrases from us but simple statements; that we don't need to prove ourselves to You; and that our persistence doesn't offend You. Lord, teach us to pray effectively. We praise You for saving us by Your mercy by the work of Your son, Jesus our Savior, and we thank You for hearing and answering our simplest of prayers. In Jesus' name, Amen.

24

Prayer + Faith = Power

When they came to the other disciples, they saw a large crowd around them and the teachers of the law arguing with them. As soon as all the people saw Jesus, they were overwhelmed with wonder and ran to greet him.

"What are you arguing with them about?" he asked.

A man in the crowd answered, "Teacher, I brought you my son, who is possessed by a spirit that has robbed him of speech. Whenever it seizes him, it throws him to the ground. He foams at the mouth, gnashes his teeth and becomes rigid. I asked your disciples to drive out the spirit, but they could not."

"Oh, unbelieving generation," Jesus replied, "how long

shall I stay with you? How long shall I put up with you? Bring the boy to me."

So they brought him. When the spirit saw Jesus, it immediately threw the boy into a convulsion. He fell to the ground and rolled around, foaming at the mouth.

Jesus asked the boy's father, "How long has he been like this?"

"From childhood," he answered. "It has often thrown him into fire or water to kill him. But if you can do anything, take pity on us and help us."

"'If you can'?" said Jesus. "Everything is possible for him who believes."

Immediately the boy's father exclaimed, "I do believe; help me overcome my unbelief!"

When Jesus saw that a crowd was running to the scene, he rebuked the evil spirit. "You deaf and mute spirit," he said, "I command you, come out of him and never enter him again."

The spirit shrieked, convulsed him violently and came out. The boy looked so much like a corpse that many said, "He's dead." But Jesus took him by the hand and lifted him to his feet, and he stood up.

After Jesus had gone indoors, his disciples asked him pri-
vately, "Why couldn't we drive it out?"

He replied, "This kind can come out only by prayer."
(Mark 9:14–29)

M any times we feel that we are in over our heads.
Maybe we have a personal problem, a family conflict, or a financial struggle, and we can't cope; whatever the
cause, we feel completely overwhelmed.

Our heart goes out to the father in this passage. The
boy was totally out of control, and the father was broken-
hearted. He was frustrated because he had been talking to
the disciples and the disciples hadn't been able to help. This
was pitiful, and he was at the end of himself.

Back home the mother may have been saying, "I can't
deal with it anymore. You go. If Jesus can help, fine, but I
don't know much about this Jesus. Who is He? There are a
lot of people saying they are the Messiah. This is too big a
miracle for anybody. Our son's convulsions are awful; he
spits out foam. He can't speak, but we can look into his eyes

and realize it is hopeless. What can we do? Nobody can help us with this."

Jesus was about a half mile off. The disciples were there, as were the scribes and the religious rulers who were looking for any opportunity to undercut Him and destroy His popularity with the people. They said sarcastically to the disciples, "All right, Your Master isn't here. Let's see if you can do miracles as Jesus said You would be able to do in His name."

Then Jesus came to the scene of this demon-possessed child. The boy's father, seeing Jesus, said, "I'm so glad You're here." He began to explain the heartache of his son's condition in desperate terms and said to Jesus, "Your disciples were not able to do anything." We don't know that Jesus was embarrassed, but it was obvious that His critics were driving a wedge between His power and His disciples' powerlessness in spite of the fact that He had given them power over disease.

There are times for all of us when we have just hit bottom. The devil knows that there are some areas he holds so strongly that these strongholds cannot be easily overthrown without prayer and the total and complete reliance on the power of God.

Now, Jesus had given authority to His disciples to "overcome all the power of the enemy" (Luke 10:19). Why couldn't they perform? Was this scene so violent and grotesque? Did they lack faith? Were they afraid of the demonic power? Did they feel overwhelmed and intimidated, as would be naturally expected?

Jesus then reminded His disciples and the crowd that everything is possible to those who believe. "Oh," the father replied, "Lord, I believe." And bursting into tears, he said again, "I do believe; help me overcome my unbelief" (Mark 9:24).

Jesus said to the demon in the boy, "Come out, you deaf and dumb spirit." Jesus was saying, "That's the last time you'll touch him." The child shrieked and fell on the ground, and when he fell, the devil pulled his bones out of place, shaking him like a child would shake a doll. The boy just lay there, looking broken and lifeless. The Lord took him by the hand and lifted him up and completely delivered him from the demon.

Charles Wesley wrote, "Hear Him, ye deaf; His praise, ye dumb, your loosened tongues employ; ye blind, behold your Saviour come; and leap, ye lame, for joy."[1]

The child safely delivered to his father, Jesus and the disciples went into a house and questioned Him, "How is it we couldn't do that? How is it possible that we were powerless?" And the Lord answered, "It's because this kind can only come out by prayer."

We sometimes deal with demonic forces, spiritual evil in the highest levels whose invisible force is beyond human power. And if we're not ready for that—if we're not praying—then we're not going to be able to stand against the methods of the devil (Eph. 6:10–18).

There is no denying the connection between prayer and faith and the power that results from them. Jesus called His onlookers that day "O faithless, unbelieving generation." Would Jesus be saying that to us today? Few would deny that there is an obvious lack of prayer and confidence in His power. In many churches, it is marginalized by programs and activities, and its priority is overlooked. Someone said, "Much prayer, much power. Little prayer, little power" because the "prayer of a righteous man is powerful and effective" (James 5:16).

Jesus told His disciples that the boy could be delivered only through prayer. Some Bible texts add the word "fasting" (Mark 9:29 KJV). Fasting can be the result of a preoccupation with prayer that forgets the need for physical nourishment or deliberate self-denial in order to express devotion and sincerity when praying. Prayer is dependence upon God. It is complete dependence when we admit, "I can't handle this, Lord. But all things are possible to those who believe. I believe You can and will."

The Bible says, "Without faith it is impossible to please God" (Heb. 11:6). He wants us to trust Him. Faith and prayer are indispensable: the more we pray, the more trust we have. And the more trust and faith we have, the more power we have, because faith is the victory that overcomes the world.

May God give us great faith, and may we combine it with prayer to overcome the evil one.

Dear heavenly Father, we confess that so frequently, we experience a lack of power in dealing just with daily pressures and constant problems. Sometimes we fear that there will be times when we will experience devastating heartache. We repent that our prayers are so weak and lacking in faith. Please hear our hearts, that we do desire to experience the power of prayer, and we ask that You would increase our faith so that when we pray, we will be more intense and passionate. In Jesus' name, Amen.

25

PRAYER AND PRESUMPTION

Ask and it will be given to you; seek and you will find; knock and the door will be opened to you. For everyone who asks receives; he who seeks finds; and to him who knocks, the door will be opened.

Which of you, if his son asks for bread, will give him a stone? Or if he asks for a fish, will give him a snake? If you, then, though you are evil, know how to give good gifts to your children, how much more will your Father in heaven give good gifts to those who ask him! (Matthew 7:7−11)

Our Father longs for us to talk to Him. Everybody knows we should pray. But we don't do it as consistently as we ought to because we don't always feel the need. Everything is comfortable for us. We have wants, but we're not at the point of desperation. This hardens the heart toward reliance upon the Lord.

We see this in Biblical Israel. The Bible says they were not thankful, and the Lord had to remind them constantly of what He had done for them. He repeatedly reminded them that He was the Creator, that all things came out of His providential hands, and that He had freed them from slavery. He reminded them of their deliverance from Egypt. Every morning He provided for them bread from heaven, baked in the ovens of the angels. The mighty act He performed for them when their backs were against the sea with Pharoah's army charging toward them was unprecedented.

And yet the people "forgot His benefits." They did not call upon Him. And because of this nonchalance, they diverted their devotion from Him to idols. Veneration is a natural tendency of the human heart; when worship is not focused on God, it will settle on some other, lesser, god.

Don't we all do the same thing? We let the blessings blind us to our constant need to depend on the Lord. That can lead us to feelings of presumption, which is a very serious sin. We assume we are fine; we lose our conscious awareness that we have a relationship with the Lord that cannot be trivialized. Daily reliance upon the Lord cannot be taken for granted. If it is, it is the sin of presumption: "Keep back thy servant also from presumptuous sins; let them not have dominion over me: then shall I be upright, and I shall be innocent from the great transgression" (Ps. 19:13).

Our Lord taught that God is more than a defender, a strong tower, a shield. He is also a judge, a ruler of nations, and an avenger. Jesus said, "He's a heavenly Father. Ask and receive, knock and it will be opened, seek and you will find." By His incarnation, Jesus revealed the Father: "Anyone who has seen me has seen the Father" (John 14:9). He reminded us of God's care, comparing it to that which a father expresses to his child. He said, "How much more will your heavenly Father do for you?"

Why do we pray? Because of our relationship with God the Father. Throughout Scripture we are addressed as "children." God recognizes that we are childlike in our dependency on Him. "Which of you, if his son asks for bread, will give him a stone? Or if he asks for a fish, will give him a snake?" Jesus asked. Your Heavenly Father knows you are related to Him, and He knows everything you need even before you ask. "How much more will your Father in heaven give good gifts to those who ask him!" (Matt. 7:9, 11).

We pray because God is our Father, and we are His. We have a right to pray to Him. He is our Savior, and He is our Redeemer. He wants us to talk to Him. The principle of prayer is, "You're My child, I'm Your Father; I want to talk to you." This relationship is the essence of prayer.

Yet His goodness becomes an excuse to neglect Him. This is why we do not pray. Because we are "blessed" we become insensitive to our need for His ongoing grace and mercy. And the sad thing then is that our relationship with God fades and seems distant. We pray only when we have to, only when it's convenient or only when we have a real need.

What's the answer to that? We should not presume on grace. We are rich in the Lord's mercy when sickness comes or in financial crises or after the unexpected tragedy. And we need to contemplate all His goodness: Read the Scripture with introspection; journal His blessing in you life so far; speak to your family and friends of His goodness; praise Him every day and remind yourself that He is ever present. He has given us so much; we are not sufficiently thankful.

Again, Jesus said to ask, seek, and knock. His commands plead with us to keep on asking, keep on seeking, keep on knocking. When we pray, our confidence increases as our love grows. We call to mind His goodness to us and our deep, perpetual need for grace.

Father, we're children. We call, remembering Your goodness to us and our deep, perpetual need for grace. Help us to depend on You and talk with You about everything in our lives. We know that You hear us and are more anxious to hear from us than so often we are to talk to You. Thank You for the awesome privilege of access to You at anytime. Forgive our presumption and renew our hearts in Jesus' holy name, Amen.

26

Six Conditions for Answered Prayer

"I will do whatever you ask in my name, so that the Son may bring glory to the Father. You may ask me for anything in my name, and I will do it.

If you love me, you will obey what I command." (John 14:13—15)

"This is love for God: to obey his commands . . . This is the confidence we have in approaching God: that if we ask anything

according to his will, he hears us. And if we know that he hears
us—whatever we ask—we know that we have what we asked of
him." (1 John 5:3, 14—15)

If we recorded our prayers, we would see that most of them are primarily just about ourselves. We keep asking and nothing happens, and we say our prayers don't work. Well, prayer works only when we comply with God's operational procedures. Only as we pray in the manner He says we should, will our prayers be effective.

We saw in the last chapter that a relationship with the Lord is the primary reason for prayer. Prayer isn't a perfunctory thing like a footnote in a book; prayer is our essential lifeline to God's throne and heart. We're in love with God. We rely on Him. The very breath we breathe comes from God. God is Lord over all. If we don't believe that all we have, all we are, and all we will be comes from the Lord, we certainly won't pray. People believe in God, but He's only an ingredient in life. Prayer is the least used means to receive God's grace. When the word prayer is mentioned, the immediate inner reactions are feelings of inadequacy, awkwardness, and even guilt. Rather than it being a desire, it seems to feel like a duty that has been neglected.

Yet prayer should be about more than our needs, our wants, or even our emergencies. Seventy times the psalmist said, "I cry unto the Lord" or "I call upon the Lord." He asked God to listen to the cries of his heart. This is a good reason to pray, but it is not the only kind of prayers we should pray.

Unless we understand what prayer essentially is, we will go to the Lord only because of what He can do for us. Our reasons will be self-centered. Let us understand God's conditions for answered prayer and learn to pray His way.

Our Lord said in the Gospel of John, "And whatsoever ye shall ask in my name, that will I do, that the Father may be glorified in the Son" (John 14:13 KJV). This promise seems, at first glance, to be like a genie in a bottle, granting our every wish. But it's not; the first condition is that we pray in His name. When we pray in Jesus' name, whatever we ask of Him must correspond with who He is. James the apostle wrote (4:3) that, if we ask God for something, we selfishly want and think we deserve it, we're not going to get it. "You consume things," James said, "in your lust." Lust is a desire that's obsessive and self-pleasing. No, God wants us to pray according to His character. If what we pray for is something Jesus would want for us, we pray correctly.

The second condition is that Jesus will answer our prayers if they glorify the Father. When I pray, I need to ask myself, "Will this and its outcome glorify God? Is He going to get all the credit? Is He going to be exalted? Is He going to be magnified? Is He going to be praised? Is He going to be worshiped? Is He going to be honored? Is He going to be pleased? Is His will going to be done?" If I pray with those qualifications in mind, God says He will always respond to my prayer.

There's a relationship between loving God and doing what He says, between our obedience and answered prayer. Isaiah 29:13 says, "These people come near to me with their mouth and honor me with their lips, but their hearts are far from me." Jesus asked, "Why do you call me, 'Lord, Lord,' and do not do what I say?" (Luke 6:46). The first and greatest commandment is to "love the Lord your God with all your heart and with all your soul, and with all your mind" (Matt. 22:37). If we put that in place, then everything else, all the other commandments, and the living out of our faith will flow from the love and devotion of our God. Consequently we do what the Lord wants us to do because love is in our hearts.

Therefore, the third condition is this: If we say we love God, we keep His commandments. If we don't keep His commandments, we don't really love Him. If we don't love Him, don't obey Him, then how do we expect to receive answers to our prayers?

James also wrote about the fourth condition for answered prayer: "When he asks, he must believe and not doubt, because he who doubts is like a wave of the sea, blown and tossed by the wind. That man should not think he will receive anything from the Lord; he is a double-minded man, unstable in all he does" (1:6–8). How does a wave of the sea act? It takes you up, takes you down, takes you up, takes you down. It's constantly shifting. If we doubt, we should expect nothing from God; faith in the Lord Jesus is the anchor of the soul (Heb. 6:19), so doubt your doubts and believe that God is able. Pray sincerely, believing without hesitation or reservation.

Fifth, our determination must be fixed. We read in Luke 18 that Jesus taught us to pray relentlessly. Pray with persistence, determination—don't give up. Keep on knocking, seeking, asking—perpetually. You don't just say a prayer, you keep it up until you get the answer. This fervency is proof of your sincerity.

Sixth, we must be forgiving. In the gospel of Matthew, Jesus gave us a model prayer in which He said. "Forgive us our debts, as we also have forgiven our debtors." And then He emphasized, "If you forgive men when they sin against you, your heavenly Father will also forgive you" (Matt. 6:12, 14). Obviously the opposite is also true: if you go to God for forgiveness yet you have not been forgiving others, what would you expect? In fact, Jesus told us to reconcile with our offender before coming to Him (Matt. 5:23–24). We need to resolve our differences with people before we can expect God to hear and answer us. Holding grudges results in bitterness and cancels our calls to heaven.

How can we become confident in approaching God in

prayer? John the apostle told us: "If we ask any thing according to his will, he heareth us . . . [and] we know that we have the petitions that we desired of him" (1 John 5:14–15 KJV). We have assurance when we follow the conditions for answered prayer. We pray what we believe He wills, we ask for what will bring Him glory, we obey His commands, we do not doubt, we ask repeatedly, and we pray from pure hearts full of forgiveness.

Father, in Jesus' name and to Your glory alone I want to do Your will and to receive all that I need by faith. May the words of my mouth and the thoughts of my heart be acceptable in Your sight for You are my Strength and my Redeemer. Amen.

27

BE BOLD IN PRAYER

Therefore, brothers, since we have confidence to enter the Most Holy Place by the blood of Jesus, by a new and living way opened for us through the curtain, that is, his body, and since we have a great priest over the house of God, let us draw near to God with a sincere heart in full assurance of faith, having our hearts sprinkled to cleanse us from a guilty conscience and having our bodies washed with pure water. Let us hold unswervingly to the hope we profess, for he who promised is faithful. (Hebrews 10:19—23)

The author of Hebrews wrote to people who were stalled in their Christian life, who were not moving forward, who had lost any spiritual momentum. They had truth as information, but they assumed they knew enough and that that was all they needed.

We never have "enough" of the Lord. If the Lord has all of us, then the Lord will give us more of Himself. If we don't hunger and thirst after righteousness, we'll become anemic and feel miserable in our Christian experience. Too many Christians resemble this. They're content with what little they know, and their joyless lives reflect it.

To know basic doctrine, just the ABCs, is not enough. Hebrews 6:1 says, "Let us leave the elementary teachings about Christ and go on to maturity." The writer was saying, "You've tasted of the Holy Spirit, and you know all of the primary principles, yet you're not growing." The author feared his readers would end up being just like the people of Israel before Jesus. They saw God do wonderful things for them, even bring them out of slavery into freedom in their own country, yet they complained, argued, and craved what was not good for them. They really wanted to reverse what God had done. They longed to be back in Egypt. Imagine! A phrase that repeats itself in Hebrews is that "there remains a Sabbath-rest for the people of God," but some are not there yet (see Heb. 4:1–11). People who procrastinate provoke God. We all need to move on. Your present level of spiritual growth is always unacceptable.

The Bible describes the problem and prescribes the antidote for this spiritual person. In Acts 4:29, we read that when the believers felt threatened and stuck, they prayed, "Grant unto thy servants, that with all boldness they may speak thy word" (KJV). Verse 31 says, "And when they had prayed, the place was shaken where they were assembled together. They were all filled with the Holy Ghost, and they spake the word of God with boldness."

To be bold is to be unashamed. How many people do we know who are bold in Christ? Do we hear bold prayers? If we are to come to the throne of grace to receive help in time of need, shouldn't we show assertiveness? As we come to Him, we come with a confidence that He hears us. Great boldness does not disregard His holiness nor is it disrespectful.

How can we be bold in prayer? God's Word says, "Having therefore, brethren, boldness to enter into the holiest by the blood of Jesus . . ." (Heb. 10:19 KJV). The "holiest" refers to the sanctuary, the dwelling place of God. Only one man, one priest, could go once a year into that room, where he could make one offering. This was on the Day of Atonement. Yet at Jesus' crucifixion, when the huge, thick veil of the temple was torn in half, He made a way that people could enter into the holiest place, the very presence of God.

Think about that! In prayer, we are in the presence of God. He's right there with us. He's in our hearts. The apostles preached that Christ is in us, the hope of glory (Col. 1:27), that our bodies are the temple of the living God (1 Cor. 6:19). If that's true, why are we not bold when we call on God? In our singing? In our praise and worship?

We can have boldness in prayer because of the blood of Christ. He's the perfect Savior. He's the glorified Intercessor. He's the reigning King. He rose from the dead, and all power in heaven and earth is His. And He offers this power to us.

There are two things we need for this confidence. First, "let us draw near" (Heb. 10:22). Eliminate all distractions. Go boldly to the throne of grace. Don't hesitate. Don't allow any distance between you and the Lord. Paul wrote, "Since we have such a hope, we are very bold" (2 Cor. 3:12).

Second, "Let us hold fast the [acknowledgement] of our faith without wavering; 'for he is faithful who promised'" (Heb. 10:23 KJV). Let us approach, and let us hang on and never let go. Faith and our confession come together. His grace secures our faith. Never let up. Never give up.

As the Scripture says, we can come confidently unto the throne of grace because of the redemption of Christ who, as our High Priest, sacrificed Himself for us. Come near. Don't shy away; don't hang back. Come to the throne often for Jesus Christ is Lord.

Heavenly Father, thank You that Your Son lived, died, and is alive again, and that we have such great assurance in coming to You in prayer. By His blood, He has cleared the way and given us confidence in Your presence. Help us, Father, to be faithful and to mature in our faith. In Jesus' name, Amen.

PART VI

THE HOLY SPIRIT:

THE KEY TO

POWER

AND PRESENCE

28

THE PERSON AND WORK
OF THE HOLY SPIRIT

We have not received the spirit of the world but the Spirit who is from God, that we may understand what God has freely given us. This is what we speak, not in words taught us by human wisdom but in words taught by the Spirit, expressing spiritual truths in spiritual words. (1 Corinthians 2:12–13)

When [the Holy Spirit] comes, he will reprove the world of sin, and of righteousness, and of judgment. (John 16:8 KJV)

It is God who makes both us and you stand firm in Christ.
He anointed us, set his seal of ownership on us, and put his
Spirit in our hearts as a deposit, guaranteeing what is to come.
(2 Corinthians 1:21–22)

But when he, the Spirit of truth, comes, he will guide you into
all truth. He will not speak on his own; he will speak only what
he hears, and he will tell you what is yet to come. (John 16:13)

The Holy Spirit is the Person of God who is "all for Jesus." Jesus said, when He comes, "He will not speak of Himself; He will glorify Me." This is the exclusive attribute of the Holy Spirit. God the Father, God the Son, God the Holy Spirit—three in one. The culmination of all that is to be known this side of eternity is finalized in the third person of the Trinity, the Holy Spirit.

What does the Holy Spirit do? First, the Spirit expresses spiritual reality in spiritual words (see 1 Cor. 2:13). It is not possible to know Jesus as Savior or understand the Scripture without the Holy Spirit.

Second, He convicts the human race of sin (John 16:8). What does it mean to convict? It means to make aware or conscious of all wrong. Guilt is a gift that leads us to grace. It's like a nerve in our bodies. A finger too close to heat feels pain. A nerve is a good thing—so is the Holy Spirit as a sensor to the soul. The convicting work of the Holy Spirit awakens, disturbs, judges, and convicts.

"Convict" means to make a judgment, as when a judge evaluates a case, then renders a decision. The Spirit does this in the conscience, in the heart. He stirs and agitates. He causes people to feel how lost and helpless they are to solve the issues of life and death, preparing the soul for the love of Jesus.

Third, the Holy Spirit places us in the family of God. He makes us permanently secure as God's children. The word "seal" means *to mark*. It is the symbol, the identification of authority by God's acceptance: "For him hath God the Father sealed" (John 6:27 KJV). Paul wrote, "Who hath also sealed us, and given the earnest of the Spirit in our hearts" (2 Cor. 1:22 KJV). It means that we have the designation that identifies us as Christ's forever. The Holy Spirit guarantees "what is to come"—eternal life.

Fourth, the Holy Spirit helps us to abide. Jesus said, "Abide in me . . . If ye abide in me, and my words abide in you, ye shall ask what ye will, and it shall be done for you" (John 15:4, 7 KJV). This is the secret to a holy life. "Abide" means to rest, reside. This is the personal enjoyment of a life in Christ.

The Holy Spirit makes hearts the home in which Jesus lives. Paul wrote, "Do you not know that your body is a temple of the Holy Spirit, who is in you, whom you have received from God?" (1 Cor. 6:19). The Holy Spirit reminds us of Jesus' words, "Abide in me."

The Holy Spirit also assures. When someone is convicted of sin, accepts Jesus as Savior, is sealed, and learns to abide in the Lord, he experiences full confidence that he belongs to God. He knows this because of the witness of the Spirit: "You received the Spirit of sonship. And by him we cry, 'Abba, Father.'" (Rom. 8:15). Abba is the first sound of a little baby before he can form the words of language. The Spirit Himself testifies with our spirit that we are God's children.

And finally, the Spirit speaks God's words to us. When we have the Spirit of God, He gives the insight to understand what God is doing or desires to do in and through us. Jesus said the Holy Spirit "will guide you into all truth" and "show you things to come." This is the forecast of coming events of prophecy (John 16:13). Personally strive to know not only what Christ did for you, but also what the Holy Spirit is doing in you and what Christ will do when He returns to evacuate His church. This knowledge gives hope, power, confidence, and urgency.

Jesus, before His ascension, said that His physical presence would be replaced by the Holy Spirit: "I have been with you; the Spirit will be with you." This gift of God's Spirit regenerates your lifeless soul, reveals who Jesus is and indwells all who receive Him. The Holy Spirit fills the life of those who know Jesus and who discover security in God's family.

> *Father, we praise You for giving Your Holy Spirit and that He reveals our need for Your Son as our Lord and Savior. We thank You for His abiding presence. We pray that He will reveal more of Jesus to us, which is His holy purpose. In Jesus' name, Amen.*

29

It's Better This Way

Now I am going to him who sent me, yet none of you asks me,
"Where are you going?" Because I have said these things, you
are filled with grief. But I tell you the truth: It is for your good
that I am going away. Unless I go away, the Counselor will not
come to you; but if I go, I will send him to you. (John 16:5–7)

When Jesus said, "It's better that I go away," how do
you think the disciples felt? Certainly frightened
by the immediate future. Everything the Savior did and said
gave them identity and affirmation. After thirty-six months

of seeing miracles, watching debates with religious leaders, listening to His teaching and preaching, and private times alone with the Master, they must have been shocked and saddened when Jesus said He would go away, back to the Father.

How could life possibly be better when He is not here? they must have wondered. And yet He said, "It will be better because of the Holy Spirit." Jesus was visible; the Holy Spirit was invisible. Jesus was tangible; the Holy Spirit was intangible. Jesus was present, but He would soon be absent. He assured them that the Holy Spirit would indwell them and accomplish greater things through them than even He did (John 14:12).

Do we ever think that things would be better if Jesus were still physically here? Think of what He could do. He could go to the hospitals and just look at people or touch them, and every one of them would be healed. He could be seen and heard globally, twenty-four hours a day by radio and satellite television. Think of how wonderful and rapid would be the spread of the gospel if Jesus did the same miracles today that He did then. The blind would see; deformity and paralysis would disappear; the dead would be raised; there would be no physical illness or disease.

How is it better that the Spirit comes to us? Well, when we are lost, He regenerates. When we are spiritually dry, He is water. When we are cold, He is fire. When we are dead, He is life. When we are divided, He unites. When we are at war, He is peace. When we are carnal, He convicts. When we are unable to pray, He intercedes. When we are visionless, He shows us things to come. When we are timid about evangelism and sharing the gospel, He is the motivator and empowers us to witness. When we are ignorant, He is the Teacher. When we are purposeless, He is the guide. When we are floundering, He leads us.

Jesus said that life with the Spirit would be better for three reasons. First, it calls for more faith. If we had a physical Jesus before us, we wouldn't need much faith; we could see Him and therefore believe in Him. The Holy Spirit is invisible; we must exercise faith to believe in Him. Jesus said to Thomas, "Blessed are those who have not seen and yet have believed" (John 20:29). Physical evidence supports and substantiates faith, but it does not initiate faith. Faith is based on what we don't see, not what we do see. Faith's focus is God, His spirit.

Put simply, Jesus' departure enhances faith; so does the invisibility of the Holy Spirit. Even though we cannot see Him, He is here; He is omnipresent. He inspired the inerrant Scriptures; He interprets the Scripture; He teaches the Scripture; He applies the Scripture. He brings conviction. All that we do and all that we are now is a result of the initiating power of the Holy Spirit.

Second, Hebrews 2:14 says, "Since the children have flesh and blood, [Jesus] too shared in their humanity so that by his death he might destroy him who holds the power of death—that is, the devil." Since Jesus Christ, God the Son, became human like us, He could then die, rise again, and vanquish Satan's enslavement of people to sin and death and hell (Rev. 1:17–18).

Satan holds people in bondage by the fear of death, but when they believe in the Lord Jesus Christ and receive His life by faith, they are "free from the law of sin and death" (Rom. 8:2).

Only with the Lord Jesus Christ is the devil's power destroyed. And only with the power of the Holy Spirit can we proclaim that Jesus is Lord (1 Cor. 12:3).

The third reason life with the Spirit is superior is expressed in Jesus' words: "As my Father hath sent me, even so send I you" (John 20:21 KJV). When He had the disciples with Him, they were simply in His entourage. Then Jesus said, "I'm going to go away, and what the Father gave to me to do, I now give you to do." When Jesus left the earth, He sent His Spirit; we now are given the authority and the power to do the work He called us to do. This is the greatest privilege and responsibility of each of us—to go into all the world with the gospel, energized by the Holy Spirit. Commissioned by Jesus, committed to His purpose, confident of His presence, and covered with His power, we can do a greater work because He is enthroned in Heaven (Heb. 1:3). Jesus said, "All power is given to me in heaven and in earth. Go ye therefore, and teach all nations, baptizing them in the name of the Father, and of the Son, and of the Holy Spirit: Teaching them to observe all things whatsoever I have commanded you: and, lo, I am with you alway, even unto the end of the world" (Matt. 28:18–20 KJV).

The Lord Jesus Christ, who created the world, who died for our sins, who rose again, and who will reign forever, said the Holy Spirit would become ours because of Him. "He lives with you and will be in you" (John 14:17). He sent the Spirit to be our constant Companion and indwelling source of comfort and power. The Word tells us that among other things, the Spirit will guide us into all truth (John 16:13), help us discern spiritual matters (1 Cor. 2:14–15), pray for us and with us (Rom. 8:26), and designate personal spiritual gifts in us (see 1 Cor. 12).

While the disciples no doubt longed for Jesus to stay with them, He promised He would send one exactly like Himself after He departed. And so today we have the Holy Spirit, who ignites our faith, breaks Satan's hold, and empowers our service.

We give all glory and honor to You, Father in heaven, for Your Son, the Lord Jesus Christ. We thank You for His death and resurrection, and with Your gift of the Holy Spirit, we can experience everything about Jesus in a deeper way than His earthly disciples. Fill us with Your Spirit so that we will express the gospel by our witness and our work. Only in Jesus' name we pray, Amen.

30

HOLY SPIRIT DOS AND DON'TS

"In him we have redemption through his blood, the forgiveness of sins, in accordance with the riches of God's grace." (Ephesians 1:7)

"Be ye kind to one another, tenderhearted, forgiving one another, even as God for Christ's sake hath forgiven you." (Ephesians 4:32)

Forgiveness is every person's deepest need and the greatest quality of being like Jesus. The premise of forgiveness is sinfulness. Where there is no transgression there is no need for forgiveness. When there is the denial of God and absolutes of right and wrong, there is no desire for forgiveness because it is presumed that there is no offense. This is the death of conscience.

The obstacle to forgiveness is that the person is unwilling to admit his offense. This is the scourge of the human race. This is why God's love and the giving of His Son to die for the sins of the world is so amazing. Christ died for the ungodly (Rom. 5:8). Forgiveness is all about Jesus and Jesus alone. God forgives only because Jesus took my sin and its judgment on the cross. He took in His body our sins so that we could live unto righteousness (1 Peter 2:24) and made us holy and without blame before Him in His love (Eph. 1:4).

Jesus tells the story of a slave who owed a wealthy man millions of dollars. When the debt was due, the slave could not pay. He was released and forgiven of all he owed. But then the slave went to another slave who owed him less than twenty-five dollars, and when he also could not pay, he had his fellow slave put in prison. The wealthy man was furious and handed over the unforgiving slave to be tormented until he should pay all he had owed. The moral of the parable was so obvious. Jesus said, "So likewise shall my heavenly Father do also unto you if ye from your hearts forgive not every one his brothers their trespasses (Matt. 18:35 KJV).

What keeps us from forgiving each other? In the first place, we are prone to focus on the problem or the wrong done to us rather than on the person who wronged us. The unforgiving slave saw only the money. Forgiveness had been extended to him, so he should have had the same attitude of compassion, as Jesus said. But he didn't.

Secondly, an unforgiving person overlooks his own failures. Jesus told the parable of a man who ignored a large piece of wood in his own eye but only noticed a speck in another man's eye. Jesus wanted to illustrate how much easier it is to blame and accuse others and ignore our own failures, and by holding a grudge, refuse to forgive others. But Jesus assumed our guilt and shame and forgave us, and He was holy, harmless, and sinless.

Thirdly, the unforgiving person always believes he has the right to judge. To condemn others, we assume we fully understand the reason for the conflict: it is obviously the other person's fault and the blame is theirs. Without an apology, there is no forgiveness.

Jesus' forgiveness of us is the reason why we forgive others. Every time we forgive others, deserving it or not, we have a reminder of God's forgiveness. The last words Jesus gave to His disciples were to preach "repentance and forgiveness of sins" sending them, knowing that they had forgiveness by His blood, and cleansing from all sin (Luke 24:47; 1 John 1:7). Of all the virtues of Jesus, of all the power in His name, there is nothing that exceeds His eternal absolution of all sin and from all judgment, His forgiveness of a person who believes and receives Him as Savior and Lord. We will forever say it is All for Jesus.

Dear Father, I cannot thank You enough for constantly forgiving me because of Jesus who died and rose again for me, and for taking away all my sins. I accept Your grace which makes this possible, empowering me to forgive others. May I always live to the praise of Your glory and to the honor of Your holy name. In Jesus' name, Amen.

NOTES

CHAPTER 9

1. Isaac Watts, "When I Survey the Wondrous Cross." Public domain.

CHAPTER 22

1. Cleland Boyd McAfee, "Near to the Heart of God." Public domain.

CHAPTER 24

1. Charles Wesley, "O for a Thousand Tongues." Public domain.

ACKNOWLEDGMENTS

A special thank you to Ross Rhoads for his faithful proclamation of the gospel. The entire crusade staff and team join me in expressing heartfelt gratitude to Ross for the in-depth preparation of daily devotionals shared each morning during weeks my father, Dr. Billy Graham, and I conduct evangelistic crusades across North America and around the world.

The most important part of the day during a crusade is our morning devotions, when all those participating in the evening meetings gather for a time of Bible study and prayer, asking almighty God for His guidance and power as His life-changing message is proclaimed.

Ross's dedication and commitment to this part of our ministry is immeasurable. As we travel around the world preaching and proclaiming the Good News, Ross helps us to focus on what God wants to do in each of our hearts. He has ministered to the entire team, and the Lord has used him to challenge and encourage. He is a valued friend and co-laborer in doing the work of an evangelist.

It is with deep gratitude to Ross and his wife, Carol, who has spent hours editing this manuscript, that I share with each reader these daily devotions that the team has been privileged to hear and take to heart.

—FRANKLIN GRAHAM
Evangelist, President, and CEO of the
Billy Graham Evangelistic Association and
President and CEO of Samaritan's Purse

ABOUT THE AUTHORS

FRANKLIN GRAHAM is President and CEO of Samaritan's Purse, a Christian relief and evangelistic organization. He is also President and CEO of the Billy Graham Evangelistic Association. Franklin is the fourth of Billy and Ruth Bell Graham's five children. He is the author of the best-selling autobiography *Rebel with a Cause, Living Beyond the Limits, The Name,* and the children's book *Miracle in a Shoebox.* An avid outdoorsman and pilot, Franklin and his wife, Jane, make their home in North Carolina and have four children, two daughters-in-law, and two granddaughters.

ROSS S. RHOADS, B.A., M.S., D.D., serves as Vice Chairman of the Board of Directors of Samaritan's Purse and World Medical Mission. He and his wife, Carol, are national representatives of Operation Christmas Child. Ross, an evangelist and retired pastor, now serves as the chaplain for Franklin Graham Ministries and the Billy Graham Evangelistic Association.